*Sue,
Your energy
is infectious! ?!
through all your Next Things!
Cecil Fayle*

The Next Thing

A Christian Model for Dealing
with Crisis in Personal Life

Inscript

Bladensburg, Maryland

The Next Thing: A Christian Model for Dealing
with Crisis in Personal Life
Copyright 2022 by Cecil Taylor

Paperback ISBN 978-1-957497-13-6

All Scripture quotations are taken from the Holy Bible, New International Version®, NIV®. Copyright © by Biblica, Inc.™ Used by permission of Zondervan. All rights reserved worldwide. www.zondervan.com The "NIV" and "New International Version" are trademarks registered in the United States Patent and Trademark Office by Biblica, Inc.™ Versions from 2022 and 1995 are used.

Inscript and the portrayal of a pen with script are trademarks of Dove Christian Publishers.

MANUFACTURED IN THE UNITED STATES OF
AMERICA

Contents

Gratitude

I am grateful for the encouragers who helped me get to this point, either through their support of this book's development and/or through their support of Cecil Taylor Ministries.

Foremost, I want to thank my wife, Sara Taylor, for her faith and bravery in volunteering to share very personal details in this book in her desire to help others. Her belief in Cecil Taylor Ministries has been vital in getting to this point and beyond.

Thanks as well to:
- Connor Walden for providing the outstanding artwork. It was completely different from "Live Like You're Loved," but just as excellent.
- Len Wilson for his guidance in the realm of publishing.
- Pat Warren and Greg Hasty for reviewing and providing feedback on this book.
- Sean Lofgren for his effervescent encouragement and for placing in my head the guiding light for my ministry, to share what I know with a hurting world that needs to hear it.

About the Author

As the son of a preacher, Cecil Taylor understands the complexity of the word "call".

A lifetime's worth of "calls" has led Cecil to successful careers in software development, broadcast radio, and product management at the forefront of the telecom industry. And yet, despite the unique journey God has led him on, the struggle he has faced his entire life is one that is shared by most Christians:

How do you reconcile your call to ministry and call to Christ with the other directions God is leading you? How do you continue to grow closer to God in love and service when you're dedicated to so many other pursuits, whether it's a career or family or just the constant grind necessary in life?

Forty years of teaching adults and youth in church has allowed God to give some answers to Cecil and move his call to sharing it further. That's what Cecil Taylor Ministries is all about: humbly passing on wisdom that God has used already to change one life, in the hopes that it changes the lives of many.

The foundation of Cecil's experience is that every day of the week can be Sunday.

The feeling of intimacy, connection, growth, and love that we find in church and in communion with Christ isn't limited to one day a week. In fact, the start of understanding your call to ministry as a Christian is learning that God is present in every direction he has called you. Your career, your family, the constant highs and lows of life, all of them hold meaning to God.

Cecil's call and the main point of Cecil Taylor Ministries is to help you and others learn about a 7-day practical faith. Cecil Taylor Ministries offers video lessons, books, study materials, podcasts, devotionals and more to help churches, small groups and individual learners understand how to live a 7-day practical faith.

At the writing of this edition, Cecil has created two video series before "The Next Thing":

"Live Like You're Loved"
The truth is that you are loved by God, forgiven by God, sent by God, and invited to eternal relationship with God. But do you believe this Bible message? If you did believe it and lived like it, how would your life change? A five-lesson series to explore living like you're loved, forgiven, sent, and eternal.

"The Legacy Tree: A Christian Model for a Life of Significance"
The Legacy Tree is a 12-lesson series that uses a tree metaphor to teach how to define ourselves, give ourselves,

and replenish ourselves to move from success to significance as we contribute to God's kingdom. It can be viewed separately in three modules of four sessions each.

For current information on the products and services available through Cecil Taylor Ministries, please visit **CecilTaylorMinistries.com.**

Introduction

I have a reason for writing this book when I mainly use other media to communicate. Cecil Taylor Ministries is my ministry venture, dedicated to teaching Christians how to live a 7-day practical faith. My normal content delivery method is video lessons, and this topic of "The Next Thing" is firstly a video lesson series.

But there is a problem with video lessons. Typically, you watch them in a group, and then the lessons are gone. You probably don't possess the videos themselves. Even if you do, there is little to remember them by, unless you watch the videos again. After a while, you may have embedded some ideas in your life, but you have no way to remember the details of what you learned or have the ability to review them again.

A book is more lasting. A book can be accessed again and again. Plus, a book can expand on ideas in a way that a time-limited video lesson cannot. In addition, the content of this book would be very useful to review again when you hit a crisis.

Because my primary purpose of spending the time and energy to write a book is to extend the video lesson experience, this book is organized differently than it would be if I started with a book and then developed video lessons. Actually, that is the way I think a lot of authors work: they write the book first, then the video lessons.

As one who usually watches the video first, I get frustrated with the write-the-book-first method. It can be hard to find what I remember from the video, buried underneath a mountain of other words. Also, the organization of book chapters may be different from the video. It feels like I have to pick through such a book to find the bits that showed up in the video. Therefore, I have organized this book with a better mapping to "The Next Thing" video series, making it easier for viewers to find in the book what they learned in the video series.

As I mentioned, a book should take you deeper into the topic, and I'll do that in The Next Thing book, with more insights, more stories, and more sources to supplement my ideas.

For those of you reading the book before watching the video series, I hope to give a thorough experience with an organization that also makes sense to book-only or book-first participants.

Another motivator in writing a book is to offer an additional way to connect to you, the reading audience, that could possibly lead to more connection. The topic of dealing with crises in your personal life is a rich one for sharing ideas and experiences. This happened within the space of groups watching the video series together, but now I hope to offer ways to expand that conversation and get more people to build upon my thoughts and experiences by adding theirs, so that we can all learn together and better address the "Next

INTRODUCTION

Things" in our lives. I would appreciate hearing your stories of crisis and of using these techniques to help you through your crisis.

The Next Thing

It was the worst day of my life. It was the day everything changed. Decades later, every single day has been colored and affected by the worst day.

And on that worst day of my life, there came a moment when my wife Sara and I were sitting in our car together. It was silent as we prepared to exit the car and walk toward an uncertain future. Sara turned to me and asked, "What are we going to do?"

And I told her, "We're going to do the next thing. And then, we'll do the next thing after that. And then the next thing after that."

You see, we were in uncharted territory, faced with situations and decisions foreign to us. All we could do was to take the next step to see where it led, and then find the next thing to do – over and over and over. And that is what we did for months, even years.

This book is named after that moment. I'll be talking about crises in your personal life and a Christian-based approach to reacting to them. It doesn't matter what your crisis is, just as it really doesn't matter what my crisis was on the worst day of my life. (However, I will tell you about that crisis later in this chapter and expand on it in future chapters).

In this book, I'll share a four-part model, designed to help you get through any crisis that you face. Along the way, I'll be sharing a variety of crises I have faced and how I applied (or in cases, didn't apply) these principles.

The Essence of Crisis

Life's hard. Put that in a screaming headline! Yes, life is difficult, and problems arise all the time. Some are run-of-the-mill problems; some are crises.

How do we define a crisis? Some definitions:
- *A time of intense difficulty, trouble or danger.* In other words, a bigger problem than normal.
- *A time when a difficult or important decision must be*

2

made. By this definition, a crisis is more than just a bigger problem than normal. A crisis also demands more of us, calling upon us to make a decision.

- *A turning point; a stage in a sequence of events at which the trend of future events is determined.* I think this definition aligns nicely with the concept of a Next Thing. You might call the Next Thing a turning point, when the crisis begins or reshapes. As we'll see, crises are not necessarily a single, linear, really big problem, although some crises are that way.

Felix Timtschenko adds these parameters to the definition of crisis:

1. It comes unexpectedly (at the level of a country, "unexpected" can also mean several weeks).
2. It has a great impact (damage).
3. It is limited in time.[1]

What are examples of crisis? A crisis might be due to health, finances, relationship, legal troubles, natural disaster. Everyone could make their own personal list from life experiences. Blogger Zarrine Flores listed hers as "immigration, divorce, the death of my father under strange circumstances, cancer, an autoimmune disorder, burnout, job loss – in that order." [2]

---

1 Timtschenko, Felix: "What Does Simplify the Crisis Mean?", https://www.linkedin.com/pulse/what-does-simplify-crisis-means-felix-timtschenko/

2 Flores, Zarrine: "9 Tips for Surviving a Personal Crisis," https://www.purposefairy.com/81088/9-tips-for-surviving-a-personal-crisis/

My definition of crisis may not be your definition of crisis, though. I may even change my own definition as life unfolds. For example, as I was writing this section, I was interrupted when Sara (who is a diabetic) had a low blood sugar reaction. I recall that the first time I had to deal with her low blood sugar, it was a crisis for me! Instead of simply providing her some juice and crackers to sufficiently raise her blood sugar, I stuffed an entire meal down her! But after thousands of low blood sugars over the course of decades, the vast majority have become routine and are not a crisis. It's only a crisis these days if I can't control the low blood sugar, and we have to call an ambulance. That hasn't happened in years.

I do want to separate crises from big decisions. For example, when Sara and I made the big decision to adopt our daughter, Rebecca, from China, that was not a crisis. Now there were a few twists and turns in the process that were very difficult and frustrating; perhaps one of those could be called a crisis. In reality, they were simply setbacks that only delayed but did not stop the adoption.

Crisis Types

For the purpose of understanding the Next Thing, I want to divide crises into types, along a couple of division lines.

The first division is by path. A crisis may be a straight path, or it could be a crooked path. To illustrate this, I'll remind you of alpine skiing events.

The fastest is the downhill. I wouldn't say the course is straight down the mountain, as there are curves and jumps. But as one announcer put it, you're trying to follow the same path as if you rolled a bowling ball down the mountain. It's a relatively straightforward path.

The slowest and most technical event is the slalom. The skier weaves in and out of gates or flags set up fairly close together. The slalom has the most twists and turns of any event.

A crisis can be like the downhill, the slalom, or something in between. The curves and gates are Next Things that you have to deal with. Sometimes they are predictable. Sometimes, well, there's fog on the mountain, and it's hard to see where the next curve or gate is coming.

A second way to divide crises is by the number of simultaneous Next Things. Here, I'll use transportation as the analogy.

Sometimes a crisis is like the subway. There is only one track, only one Next Thing going on. At other times, a crisis is like a traffic jam, with multiple Next Things running in lanes side by side, competing for your attention and prioritization.

Another way to think of it is that you can have a new crisis either within, or side by side with, an existing crisis. I've seen the term "nested crises." An example: Since the COVID-19 pandemic crisis spread widely in the United States during an election year, there were calls to provide more options on how to vote. This spawned a new, divisive, parallel crisis over voting regulations that lasted well beyond Election Day 2020.

At times throughout this book, I'll refer to a crisis being a "downhill" or "slalom" crisis, or a "single-track" or "multiple-track" crisis.

Acceptance of Crisis

One of the main things we must do to effectively address a crisis is to accept it. This is harder than you may think.

First, few humans relish problems. As M. Scott Peck puts it in The Road Less Traveled, we don't want to accept that life is difficult.

> **Instead, (people) moan more or less incessantly, noisily or subtly, about the enormity of their problems, their burdens, and their difficulties as if life were generally easy, as if life *should* be easy…Life is a series of problems. Do we want to moan about them or solve them?…**

THE NEXT THING

**What makes life difficult is that the process of confront-
ing and solving problems is a painful one. Problems,
depending upon their nature, evoke in us frustration or
grief or sadness or loneliness or guilt or regret or anger
or fear or anxiety or anguish or despair.[3]**

As a result, it happens often that we want to deny that a crisis
exists; this can delay our response or make our response less
effective. I worked for nearly a decade for a Japanese high tech
company whose culture it was to deny that a crisis was emerging,
thus delaying the response. In the fast-moving world of high
tech, delaying a response was potentially calamitous. After
observing this behavior for awhile, a new member of the company
commented, "We spend a lot of time admiring the problem."

On the other hand, readily accepting a crisis and addressing
the Next Thing in front of you can be very effective. Let me
give you an example of a brief but bizarre crisis that was
effectively handled simply by accepting that it was happening.

 My wife, daughter and
I were driving on an
interstate highway out
in the country when a
crazy thing happened:
A bird flew through the
windshield! The beak of

---

3 Peck, M. Scott, *A Road Less Traveled: A New Psychology of Love, Traditional Values
and Spiritual Growth.* New York: Simon & Schuster, 1979.

the bird hit the windshield at just the right angle to puncture the windshield, and the poor little bird died, wedged halfway in, halfway out. (Later, the adjuster and the repair company representative both said they had never seen this happen in a combined 35 years of analyzing auto damage).

At impact, a lot of things happened at once in my mind.

- First, what just happened? I realize that the bird is not coming through any farther, and I could see around it to drive. I notice that the windshield was badly damaged.
- So I'm thinking, OK, life just changed. The windshield is toast. Can I drive like this to make the 70 miles back home? No, it's probably going to collapse at highway speeds, so I need to pull over.
- With shattered glass spread all the way from the dashboard to the very back of the SUV, and a lot of it on me, I'm wondering, is anyone hurt? I glance at my wife – she's apparently OK. I hear my daughter screaming in amazement in the back seat, but she seems uninjured. I feel like I have some small cuts on me, and I did, but luckily I was uninjured – you can imagine the tragedy that would have happened if I had been somehow incapacitated by this bird or the flying glass.

I slow down and pull to the shoulder, but I realize the car is running fine, and the windshield seems to be holding – for now. I see an exit and a truck stop a mile away, so I decide to get back in the right lane and drive to safety.

I asked my family later, "What did I say during that time?" They replied, "Nothing!" I was so focused that I didn't even speak or react verbally! Meanwhile, Sara said as things raced through her mind, she kept coming back to the phrase, "There's a bird in our windshield!"

The crucial moment was the realization and acceptance that I wasn't going to be able to drive normally anymore, accepting that life had changed, realizing that the windshield was too unstable to get home or even much farther than the next exit. And this is the key point of my story: The simple but critical thinking I was doing, was based on the acceptance that life has just changed. I don't want this situation, but it's here, I'm going to make the best of it, I'm going to get to a safe place, and then we'll think about Next Things such as damage and a tow truck and how we're going to make it back home.

In addition to accepting the crisis, I was using a technique of Simplifying, which takes us to the four-part model of this book.

The Next Thing Model

There are four components of this model, this response to crisis, that help you through whatever your next thing is: Simplify....Trust....Rest...and Grieve. We:

- Simplify to focus on the Next Thing.
- Trust that God and others will help you get through the Next Thing.

- Rest, so you are ready for the Next Thing.
- Grieve, so you can accept and act on the Next Thing.

These elements may seem simple, but in reality, the execution is difficult. We tend to NOT do these things when under pressure. I have applied them in my life and benefited. When sharing these techniques with others, people have resonated with them. So now I share them with you.

In each of the upcoming component chapters, I'll start with a story, much like the one I began at the start of this opening chapter. I'll describe a Practical Faith approach to enacting the component, using examples from my life and from others' lives. Then I'll turn to the Bible to provide some "scriptural wrapping paper" to place around the Practical Faith concepts. While I will use a number of scripture passages in each chapter, there will be one Core Passage that I'll primarily lean on. Each component chapter will end with a summary of the chapter, so that you can quickly refer to the model's concepts.

Before I present the component chapters, there is a promise to keep, telling you about the crisis that triggered the worst day of my life.

The Worst Days of Our Lives

Even though it's not **necessary** for you to know, Sara and I have decided to tell you what the crisis was on the worst day of my life, because we believe it's a vital topic to discuss. The crisis was that Sara had experienced the worst day of **her** life the day before: She had tried to commit suicide. On this worst day of **my** life, I was fully realizing that the overdose of the day before was intentional, and medical personnel instructed me to take her to a psychiatric hospital. When we were sitting in the car together, we were parked outside the psychiatric hospital, about to enter an unknown world and its procedures, and not knowing what would happen when they locked the door behind Sara.

The overdose was the first of numerous attempts on her life and the start of a shattered illusion, as Sara had secretly held her depression in for decades and seemed normal on the outside. But on the inside, she was doing quite terribly.

Mental health is a tremendous issue with a substantial stigma attached to it. It also affects a person's overall health, as the mind is interconnected with the body. And mental illness causes significant stress for those around the person.

It's estimated that one in six people in our country suffer from mental health issues, which means it's very likely someone reading this book is affected, either for themselves or due to a loved one. As a society, we need to be more open about mental health because you feel such shame when you're not mentally healthy. Sara urged me to be open within this book about her story, in the brave desire to help others. If you or someone you know is struggling with mental health, we pray that you're inspired by our openness to become open yourself, and we pray that you receive love and respect in dealing with your mental health crisis.

Simplify

On the worst day of my life, sometime before that moment when Sara and I were sitting in the car, I dropped off my daughter at our church's preschool. Outside, I ran into Reverend Doctor Leighton Farrell, who had baptized our daughter and was a legendary pastor in our area long before he became executive pastor of our church.

When Leighton greeted me with a cheerful "How's it going?", I told him, "Leighton, I'm having the worst day of my life." He invited me to stop back by when I had time.

Sitting in Leighton's office after admitting Sara to the psychiatric hospital, I spilled out everything that was going on. He listened very carefully. At the end, I was waiting on some words of wisdom. I was sure Leighton had seen almost every situation in ministry and could draw from that experience to tell me what to do next to specifically solve MY situation.

Leighton said, "I have some advice for you," and I eagerly waited. Then he simply said, "Stay spiritually strong."

And that was it! I felt like saying, wow, I went through all those details, and all you've got is this simple phrase, stay spiritually strong?

But it turns out, that simple advice was perhaps the best advice I ever received.

Because during the next year, I had dark thoughts that had never crossed my brain before. I was tempted in ways I had never experienced before or since. It wasn't the attractiveness of the temptations themselves; it was simply because I was angry and frustrated and scared and wanted to lash out in some way.

I recall one late evening after my wife and kids were asleep. I wanted to leave the house; I wanted to go do something completely out of character. Instead, I shut myself in a closet and kept thinking in prayer about what Leighton had said: "Stay spiritually strong."

Some days, I wanted to pick up the kids and leave. But I noticed how the psychiatric hospital was populated by a number of women whose husbands had left them at the first sign of mental illness. I was determined to fulfill, "…in sickness and in health," as well as to demonstrate faithfulness to our three children. I didn't want to display to them that if someone has become less useful to me, if someone doesn't do things the way I want, then I would discard them, because my kids could worry that they might be that someone someday.

I felt like Job at times. While I didn't believe that God had literally handed us over to Satan, I was convinced of this: Our family had exhibited strong faith and glorified God in many ways. Now it felt like we were under attack from Satan, who wanted to tear us down, destroy our faith and render us ineffective for God's kingdom. It made me more determined to not give in, and to "stay spiritually strong."

"Stay spiritually strong" was my simple approach to handling possibly the most complex situation of my life.

The Focus of Simplicity

Let me be clear that I'm not recommending a single slogan to get you through the Next Thing. Instead, the focus of simplicity is vital in all sorts of ways in a crisis.

When you are faced with crisis like I was, and you can only think of the Next Thing, a great guideline is to **simplify**.

15

Streamline. Peel away the density of the situation. Try to get back to basics. And apply repeatedly in many forms.

It's important at this point to say that LIFE isn't simple. A CRISIS isn't simple. But you can choose to simplify. Simplification implies choosing what's important. In this case, I recommend simplifying in order to focus on the Next Thing.

Here's an example. Most of us have used Google. It has perhaps the simplest home page ever, basically a decorated search bar, with only a few options tucked around the upper corners of the page. Undoubtedly this simplicity is one of the appeals of Google and has helped it become the most used search engine in history.

But this example isn't about that home page's success, but its origin. In 1998, founders Sergey Brin and Larry Page were consumed with writing code for their search engine. Brin didn't want to be distracted with trying to come up with a fancy home page like competitors Yahoo and MSN. Plus, no one in the startup company was experienced in web page design. So Brin threw together something simple to get users started and went back to designing the complicated search engine.[4]

Google's founders were focused on their Next Thing, the main thing they had to have, a world class search engine. They

---

4 Tischler, Linda: "The Beauty of Simplicity," https://www.fastcompany.com/56804/beauty-simplicity

streamlined, peeled away complexity, and did just enough to get by in other areas. This is the kind of simplifying thinking we'll use in this chapter.

Implementing Practical Faith

Now I want to share some practical faith approaches that help us simplify. The theme of Cecil Taylor Ministries is to teach Christians to live a 7-day practical faith; in other words, how to put faith into practice.

As mentioned earlier, I will show you the scriptural underpinning toward the end of each chapter, after sharing practical faith concepts. Let me explain what I mean when I say "practical faith".

"Practical faith" doesn't mean I spew Bible verses into every situation. Instead, it's about establishing a context and then living life based on that context. You'll find that my practical faith suggestions could potentially be used by non-Christians, because they are sound ideas. The reason is that, to me, Jesus gives us a very practical way to live life. He gives us a revolutionary context that doesn't agree with the rest of the world, but when we live in that context, we can take on what the world has to offer. Ultimately, any practical faith suggestions should portray a very sturdy way of living your life, built on the rock of Jesus.

I think of the Biblical role model of Joseph. Joseph didn't have fantastic encounters with God like his ancestors Abraham,

Isaac and Jacob. Joseph winds up living in a secular world in Egypt, where God encounters Joseph in a different way, through inspiration and through Joseph's humble faith and reliance on God. Joseph may appear like a wise secular man who governs the people in practical ways, but his context is that he is truly a man of God.

What do I mean in the previous two paragraphs by "context?" I have a relative who, while ethical, is an atheist. I love him and respect his opinions. He has watched my family stand up to many challenges over the years. He has seen the faith that we have used in health crises, during unemployment, and in other crises. One day he said to me, "Your family has always been strong because your family has a certain....context." I felt like he didn't want to say, "Your faith in God has been good to you!" Instead, he used the word "context."

Yet I like that word a lot. In this book and in other books and video lessons to follow, I'll be sharing practical faith ideas, but they all emerge from a certain context, as a disciple of Christ, as one who sees beyond the earthly, as one inspired by the Holy Spirit, as one who is accountable to God and to neighbor. If it's hard to immediately see how any practical faith ideas tie to scripture, I hope to create that Biblical linkage in the back part of each component chapter.

To illustrate practical faith ideas in this book The Next Thing, I will use various examples from my life. A primary example is a

 family crisis that occurred in 2020 during the COVID pandemic, when Sara's mother Ruth went into hospice care for cancer and died shortly thereafter.

Compared to most crises, the sequence of "Next Things" for this one was fairly simple and predictable. The details contained some twists and turns, but pretty quickly after she entered the hospital, it was clear what the Next Things would be. After the hospital visit would come hospice care, followed by a funeral, followed by working through grief while also managing her estate. In the vernacular I introduced earlier, this was a downhill crisis (not a slalom), with multiple lanes to consider.

Here are simplification principles we used during the crisis of the end of Ruth's life.

Practical Faith Principle: Make it Easy on Yourself

The first principle is to make things easy on yourself, as much as possible. Find help. Delegate to others. Arrange someone else to drive your kids to practice. Order takeout! Making it easy on yourself could be a small thing: not chasing perfection, leaving something undone, or doing something for which your future self will thank your present self.

To my primary example of our crisis with Ruth's health, she lived in a distant state, so Sara and I traveled and stayed at her house in a town of 15,000.

This was during a time of lockdown. Sara could only visit her mother in the hospital for one hour a day. We had plenty to do in the remaining time as we had to get things under control. There were two main tasks: Finding a hospice facility, and taking over Ruth's affairs such as paying bills.

But we had a logistics problem. Ruth's house had terrible cell reception and no Internet service. It was hard to talk in person at that stage of the pandemic. We couldn't go to a coffee shop for Internet, because you couldn't just sit in a coffee shop; it was the era of takeout or delivery only. Taking phone calls from the street corner or a grocery parking lot got old quickly. Even then, I had to drive around that parking lot for awhile to locate a good signal!

We needed a command center in order to execute our two main tasks, so our first pursuit was Internet and WiFi phone service in the house. That was the simple building block we needed in order to find and call hospice facilities and billing departments. We had to make things easy on ourselves in order to deal with the crisis.

Practical Faith Principle: Prioritize the Essential over the Optional

The next simplification principle is prioritization: Identifying and executing the essential ahead of the optional. Here's an example that isn't a crisis but shows the principle well.

I have conducted a lot of international business travel to countries like South Korea (pictured). An impending overseas trip really makes you consider the essential vs. the optional.

A week before the trip, my to-do list is <u>so</u> long. I am too ambitious. There are so many things I feel like I have to do before I leave the country. But reality sets in day by day of what can really get done.

You should see the list a day or two before the trip! By then it is VERY focused on just getting the essential things done! The optional things are either worked around or postponed until my return. I begin to come to grips with what is truly essential and what is truly optional.

As I said, we simplified during Ruth's crisis to prioritize hospice and business affairs. There were future items to consider regarding funeral and estate, and they were certainly a shadow lurking over us. Sara and I had never been in charge of a funeral. Neither of us had experience with estate procedures. But because they were in the future, and we had enough on our plate to start, they could wait for awhile.

As I was writing this book, I encountered someone who had recently completed cancer treatment. She complained that during her treatment, people were telling her all kinds of things to do, proposing a more complicated life. Instead, she prioritized what was right in front of her, putting her head down and focusing on a simple approach to take care of the essential. She said she resonated with what I've written here about simplification.

Practical Faith Principle: Clear Your Calendar

The third principle is to clear your calendar. Turn down opportunities or appointments you would normally engage in.

In Ruth's crisis, I continued working my day job remotely with that newly installed Internet service, but dramatically scaled back my hours, skipped some meetings, and handed off work to others. I was just cranking up my ministry on the side and regretted that I had to turn down a wonderful opportunity; I just couldn't see how I could commit, given the uncertainty in my family and in my schedule.

I'm not good at clearing my calendar. I'm a Type A, and I resonate with the Type A description, "Tries to cram more and more into less and less time." Yep, that's me in the mirror!

But I've been blessed that at various times in my life, I have felt a whisper from the Holy Spirit: "Clear your calendar." And each time, I have started the process of clearing my calendar and turning down new opportunities. And each time, I later found out why, as a crisis would come up that would require a ton of my attention. Usually it was a family matter, so I created space in advance to take care of my family.

I'm not saying the Holy Spirit will always be your calendar keeper! (For example, in the case of Ruth's crisis, I received no advance whisper notice). Either way, in a crisis, we need to be proactive in clearing our calendars in order to simplify our lives and focus on the Next Thing.

Practical Faith Principle: Focus on Just the Next Thing

Finally, you can simplify by focusing on the next thing in front of you. The crisis is too big to take it on all at once.

The bigger the crisis, the more the uncertainty. Humans crave certainty and don't deal well with uncertainty. Our minds can get overwhelmed with all the possible outcomes.

On the worst day of my life, and in the days, weeks and months that followed, I found it nearly impossible to anticipate the twists and turns that would happen. I couldn't predict this will happen, then this, then this. I was in a very reactive mode. There was no clear game plan to instruct us on how to get through a mental health crisis.

One of the biggest issues in the first year of Sara's depression was finding the right cocktail of medications to address her illness. With depression, "your mileage may vary," so it's a very individualized process that needs repeated tuning. It was always one step forward, one or two steps back. Optimism that proved to be false hope. A time of freedom and a bit of normalcy, followed by Sara returning to a psychiatric hospital.

In retrospect, I wish I could've done more for the kids' well-being. We did provide counseling for the older ones to help them understand what was going on and to tend to their needs, but it wasn't enough and certainly not long enough to address everything they experienced.

Still, I have to remember that in a crisis, your response is not going to be perfect. You have to get through the day. You have to get through the Next Thing. (In our case, there were a raft of Next Things that first year). Some things naturally must fall by the wayside. Do the best you can, but simplify and focus on just the Next Thing, because it alone is large enough to consume you.

I just came across the most extreme example of this concept. In April 2022, storms with high winds swirled across Texas south of Dallas-Ft. Worth, with tornadoes a possibility. Lightning struck a pallet yard in Alvarado. The resulting fire quickly spread through rows of wooden pallets, some stacked as high as 30 feet.

Next door, Lynn Dykes watched the fire spread and knew his house could be next. While firefighters made their way to the site, Dykes used a garden hose to fight the flames that edged closer to his yard. Dykes felt like he was burning alive; he saw his backyard thermometer registering 180 degrees!

Despite firefighter efforts, flames crept along his fence. Fire charred one side of his boat. Next door, a tractor-trailer melted.

Then the unthinkable happened: A tornado appeared about an hour after the fire started. Firefighters ran for cover, some fleeing entirely.

"I couldn't focus on the fact I just saw a tornado in my own backyard," Dykes told *The Dallas Morning News*, "because I had to pick which thing to fight. And I chose the fire coming straight for my life."[5]

The storm passed, and the house was saved, although the pallet fire continued for days.

Talk about focusing on just the Next Thing! Lynn Dykes had his hands full of Next Things, but he did the right thing. The fire was almost certain to engulf him and his home. The tornado loomed, but it wasn't actually in his back yard – yet, if ever. Dykes focused on just the Next Thing and not the other frightening possibility.

Have you dealt with a "fire" while the "tornado" loomed? Most likely! That is often the essence of crisis. But this principle helps: Focus on the "fire" in front of you, and don't get caught up with the "tornado" that may or may not arrive soon.

---

5 Landers, Jamie. *The Dallas Morning News*, April 6, 2022.

As with all the practical faith principles in this chapter, this is a principle where other people can help you simplify. They have an objective view. Seeing things from the outside, they can clear your head and help you focus on the most essential, on the next thing.

If I could summarize these four principles, I would use the phrase, "There are always alternatives." The best boss I ever had, Randy Birge, used to say this. He also said, "We may not <u>like</u> the alternatives, but there <u>are</u> alternatives." In a crisis, with the Next Thing rearing up in front of you, you must seek alternatives to make it easy on yourself, prioritize the essential over the optional, clear your calendar, and focus solely on the Next Thing.

I hope you can see some of the benefits of simplifying during a crisis.
- Allows us to zero in on the core issues.
- Gives us endurance; by simplifying, we can better outlast the crisis.
- Alleviates paralysis.
- Helps us cope, leading to a more peaceful, steady feeling.

How Not to Do It

I don't want you to go through this book and think I have mastered life. Well, I have mastered a few things, but it was hard-won experience that got me there. I didn't realize these

Next Thing principles until I had gone through a number of personal crises.

I'm thinking of a time that I would really like to celebrate as a huge success for holding things together during a crisis, but I can't. It was during the year after the birth of our second child, Austin.

To understand this story, I have to first tell you that Sara and I had some insurance misfortune right when Austin was conceived. Sara was carrying our insurance at the time, and there was a foul-up in the small company where she worked. They were switching insurance plans and wound up with a coverage gap of a couple of weeks. Sure enough, we unexpectedly got pregnant during that time! Of course, neither the old nor the new insurance company intended to pay for the pregnancy.

Meanwhile, I was running my own small business and had just started a really good venture that I didn't want to lose. But I also needed a bigger salary and hopefully insurance that would agree to cover the pregnancy. I was able to achieve both goals two weeks before Austin arrived. I accepted a new job that was going to take a lot of overtime, but I was still going to try to keep the new venture going on the side.

The delivery was difficult. In fact, Austin nearly died, and Sara was thought to be in danger of both liver failure and a heart attack. She was very sick for the next year.

It was left to me to handle all the overnight baby awakenings, get our toddler Anthony re-toilet-trained, care for the house, work 60 hours per week at the new job, and keep elements of my side business going, especially that new venture.

I wasn't good at clearing my calendar. I kept one aspect of my side business going too long, and I wound up deeply disappointing customers. I struggled to learn the complex technical aspects of my new job and was convinced they were going to fire me for poor performance. I continued to volunteer with the youth at my church, which did get me out of the house. But I wound up making an embarrassing mistake as part of a youth rally, and that led to me finally taking a break from youth ministry. Interestingly, at the time, I didn't see my mistake in the context of the total stress I was under. It took a long while before I understood that.

Let's take stock:
- I didn't make it easy on myself. We did have some understanding neighbors who helped out with a few family items. But otherwise, I made it so hard on myself by not acknowledging the crisis enough. (Remember, in the prior chapter, I talked about the importance of accepting the crisis. I kept fighting the fact we were in crisis).
- I neither prioritized well nor cleared my calendar. As a result, I experienced breakdowns and uncharacteristic mistakes.

- I certainly didn't focus just on the Next Thing. I was actually juggling multiple Next Things, but I simply didn't clear the deck of lower priority items until forced to do so, due to failure.

I got through it by gritting my teeth, through the sheer energy of relative youth, and yes, through some outcrying prayer. As you can see, if I had to do it all over again, I would have sent this book backward through a time portal and read this book first!

Core Passage: 2 Timothy 2: 1, 3-4

Now I want to supplement the preceding practical faith section and its context with scriptural backing – put these ideas into a box, and cover it with a "scriptural wrapping paper." Here is our core Bible passage, 2 Timothy 2: 1, 3-4, to address Simplifying.

> **You then, my son, be strong in the grace that is in Christ Jesus.**
> **...Endure hardship with us like a good soldier of Christ Jesus.**
> **No one serving as a soldier gets involved in civilian affairs – he wants to please his commanding officer.**

To be clear, Paul is urging Timothy to ministry. But the principles of endurance through hardship are something we can apply to this topic of crisis and the Next Thing.

Let me go through verse by verse to map to the Next Thing concepts I've shared so far.

Verse 1: You then, my son, be strong in the grace that is in Christ Jesus.

This is an echo of the idea to stay spiritually strong, leaning on the strength of Jesus.

It was not his own, limited, and inadequate strength that Timothy was to draw upon, but the fathomless and immeasurable strength of God alone – which is poured out in rich abundance on those that, by faith, are in union with Christ and maintaining close fellowship with the Father.

God has promised to supply sufficient strength for the tasks we are to undertake, not because of anything that we have done to deserve it, but through the unmerited and unconditional grace that has become our portion in Christ Jesus, our Lord.[6]

Verse 3: Endure hardship with us like a good soldier of Christ Jesus.

This verse has a couple of focal points. First, the idea of enduring hardship. When someone enlists in the military, they head to basic training, where they are physically and mentally conditioned for the tasks ahead. They must learn

---

6   https://dailyverse.knowing-jesus.com/2-timothy-2-1

to be obedient, to understand their duty and their role, but as much as anything, they learn to endure hardship. They learn to suffer.

I've never served in the military, but I did play football for six years from grades 7 through 12. Football prepared me for life in a way few things have. I gained a physical toughness despite typically being the smallest player on the team. I played through injuries and wounds. I only missed one game in six years, because someone stepped on my toe, and I lost the toenail. The doctor made me sit out. I came back after a week even without a toenail fully in place. My position coach took a look at my toe, spit his chewing tobacco, and said, "I don't think Taylor feels pain like the rest of us!"

I gained a mental toughness that has served me well throughout life – in hardship in business, in family struggles, in volunteer activities. I learned in football how I could push myself to another level, that there was more within me than I thought.

One offseason, the coaches put us through new drills to prepare us to play at a higher level. There was a segment of drills in the field and a segment in the weight room. The first day we did the field segment, most of us were vomiting from the effort. That was in January. By May, we could alternate, doing two segments in the field and two in the weight room, in a 40-minute period, and make it through well. Yes, there was physical toughness gained, but just as much mental toughness.

Paul writes in another passage, in Romans 5: 3-5, that suffering produces endurance or perseverance; endurance produces character; and character produces hope. Our suffering in crisis develops our ability to endure hardship, as Paul beseeched Timothy. But that endurance doesn't exist for its own sake. Endurance changes us, developing our character. Just as football gave me mental toughness to pair with physical toughness, endurance gives us a new moral and ethical quality. Finally, a developed character gives us the wherewithal to meet other situations in life, producing hope – hope that we can withstand whatever life has thrown at us.

Again, for the Christian, all this occurs in a certain context. It's not only a development of the human being, but the human soul, because we are inspired, guided, comforted and loved by the Holy Spirit as we traverse this process from suffering to hope.

That leads me back to the second part of the passage, becoming a good soldier of Christ Jesus. These attributes we gain, this context in which we live, are then applied to the tasks that Jesus sets before us. We are deployed into the world as soldiers of the cross. Of course, we're not there to literally kill; the analogy is closer to that which Paul uses in Ephesians 6, where he urges us to put on the full armor of God in order to conduct spiritual warfare against the evil powers of the world and spiritual realm. **"For our struggle is not against flesh and blood, but against the rulers, against the authorities,**

against the powers of this dark world and against the spiritual forces of evil in the heavenly realms."

I return so often to the words of C.S. Lewis in <u>The Screwtape Letters,</u> in which the demon Screwtape tells his apprentice Wormwood how every event of life either draws the human closer to God or closer to Satan. This gives us a different perspective on The Next Thing. How will this event draw us closer to God or closer to Satan? We must be equipped like a soldier for that battle for our soul's affection and focus, preparing to endure hardship until the battle is fully secured.

<u>Verse 4</u>: No one serving as a soldier gets involved in civilian affairs – he wants to please his commanding officer.

Roman soldiers followed this rule. The Roman code of Theodosius said: "We forbid men engaged on military service to engage in civilian occupations." William Barclay wrote, "A soldier is a soldier and nothing else; the Christian must concentrate on his Christianity. That does not mean that he must engage on no worldly task or business. He must still live in this world, and he must still make a living; but it does mean that he must use whatever task he is engaged upon to demonstrate his Christianity."[7]

The Christian's commanding officer, of course, is Christ. Our aim is to please God, in whatever venture we undertake,

---

7 Barclay, William. "The Letters to Timothy, Titus and Philemon". Philadelphia: Westminster Press, 1960.

but also when dealing with The Next Thing. As Thomas Constable wrote:

> **As an ordinary soldier must be single-minded in his purpose, rigorous in his self-discipline, and unquestioning in his obedience, so must every soldier of Christ.**[8]

Takeaways from the Core Passage

Based on all of the above, let me summarize the takeaways from the core passage, paired with the Practical Faith discussion before it.

First, we are to **stay spiritually strong**. This has a double meaning. As in my personal narrative, it means to avoid temptation and to remain true to your Christian character. As in the Bible study section, it also means leaning on the Lord to stay spiritually strong. That strength comes from the grace of Christ Jesus, empowering us to do His will.

Second, we are to **practice mental discipline**. Like a soldier must have mental discipline, the Christian must also exercise mental discipline when faced with The Next Thing. In the Practical Faith discussion, I gave several ideas for simplifying, which is an example of practicing mental discipline.

Third, we are to **please the Lord**, our commanding officer. I don't want to lose Paul's perspective that in every circumstance,

---

8   Constable, Thomas. "Thomas Constable's Notes on the Bible: Volume X". Hurst, TX: Tyndale Seminary Press, 2017.

every crisis, every pleasurable or distasteful situation, we should remain focused on pleasing the Lord. We need to focus on the next thing in front of us, but the Next Thing should never stop our obedience to God as we go through the crisis.

Obedience is more easily executed when we trust God. That's the subject of the next component of this four-part Next Thing model.

Summary of Simplify

Big Thought:
Simplify in a crisis to focus on the Next Thing.

Core Passage:
2 Timothy 2: 1, 3-4: "You then, my son, be strong in the grace that is in Christ Jesus…Endure hardship with us like a good soldier of Christ Jesus. No one serving as a soldier gets involved in civilian affairs – he wants to please his commanding officer."

Practical Faith ideas:
- Make it easy on yourself.
- Prioritize the essential over the optional.
- Clear your calendar.
- Focus on the Next Thing.

Guiding thoughts for crisis, based on the core passage:
- Stay spiritually strong.
- Practice mental discipline.
- Please the Lord.

Trust

Frustrated. Helpless. Mad, but more sad than mad. Those were some of my feelings as I realized – again and for the umpteenth time – that I could not control the ramifications of Sara's depression.

Many years after those worst days of our lives, even after many ups and downs and medications and counseling sessions and restarts and do-overs, it seemed like we were not much further along than we were in the first few years.

I had started to learn that when people would ask, "How is Sara doing?" and I said, "Great!," then trouble was just around the corner. I got to where I didn't want to tell people how she was, almost superstitious that I would bring on another negative episode just by speaking positively!

In reality, sometimes in the times that seemed the best, she was hiding the most, faking happiness, returning to the illusion we had before her first suicide attempt.

It was in those moments of frustration and helplessness that I realized – again – that we were dealing with an illness that Sara couldn't really control, and I certainly couldn't control! Through my contemplation and our conversations, I realized how little control I had.

When I can't control something, it means I need to walk in the other direction, toward trust. Trusting in God to hold the situation in His hands, to inspire the doctors, to walk closely with Sara. Not just to control her behaviors, but to also control my behaviors and my responses.

It shouldn't take getting to the end of your rope before you start to trust in the midst of crisis. What if we found a way to trust from the very beginning?

In this session, I'm talking about the second component for responding to crises, when all you can do is the next thing. And that is trusting that God….and others…will help you get through the Next Thing.

We talk about trusting God in a crisis, but what does that really mean? How do we break it down? Obviously, we want a good outcome, but God is trustworthy and true even when we don't receive the outcomes we want. What does it mean for us to trust God when our prayers seemingly aren't answered?

In this chapter, I want to start by defining what it means to trust God in crisis. When faced with the Next Thing, we need God to guide us. Some of that will come through direct inspiration. But a good portion will come from other people, people that we believe have been provided by God to help us.

Twists and Turns

I wrote earlier in the book about the different types of crises. Sara's depression story was the slalom type, full of twists and turns. I mentioned some of this in an earlier chapter, but now I want to lay out a clearer picture of that first year.

For the first 18 years of our marriage, we lived an illusion – an illusion that Sara was not depressed. This illusion was disrupted by her suicide attempt, and there was a Next Thing for us to deal with. The chart below shows the first turn of the journey.

Sara entered a psychiatric hospital, where a new Next Thing presented itself. Despite the hospital's precautions, Sara found a creative way to try to kill herself again. Undoubtedly, her first suicide attempt was not a one-time oddity. There was a very destructive force within Sara that we clearly had to deal with, and so there was a new Next Thing to face, as shown below.

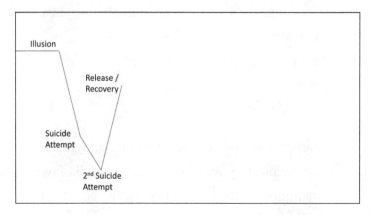

After she exited the hospital, there was about a month where she entered a new regimen of aftercare. Things seemed a little rosier yet still shaky. But it was still devastating when a third suicide attempt sent her back into the psychiatric ward.

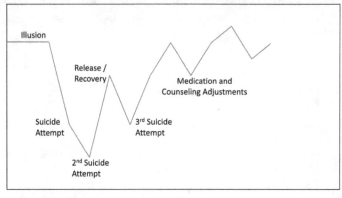

After her release, there was a period of real ups and downs that can't adequately be graphed. There were a lot of adjustments, setbacks, seemingly going in circles, mood swings, erratic behavior, and chaos as a Sara 2.0 emerged, not returning to the illusion, but trying to identify now who she really was.

At about the one-year anniversary of her first suicide attempt, there was a fourth, which led to us changing doctors and facilities in search of better answers.

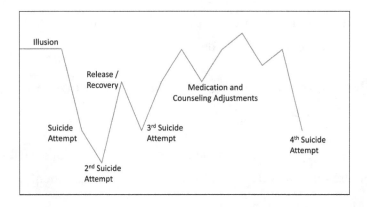

This was just the first year of Next Things, new phases to a complex illness. Many Next Things have followed, with periods of calm followed by rough periods again, with yes, more suicide attempts along the way.

As you can see, the diagram is not too different from a slalom skier's path down the hill (if flipped on its side). We experienced a high degree of unpredictability; as you can understand, this made for a chaotic family life. But there was no one-size-fits-all

41

chart of how depression would go. While there are patterns, there is substantial variability for each patient.

You're probably wondering, how is Sara doing today? Well, much better in many ways. She has matured and is in better control. She engages with consistent medical help. Sara is such a blessing to me and to others. But.....BUT....you know I don't want to sound too positive, because depression never goes away. It's a daily disease. As you've seen, depression is a series of unpredictable Next Things in an ongoing crisis. That's why I said in the beginning, those worst days of our lives have colored every day thereafter.

Practical Faith Principle: Trust the People God Sends You

Let me step back now to the crisis when Sara's mother Ruth entered her final days. And was trust ever needed then!

When Ruth went into the hospital and soon after, hospice care, it wasn't possible to ask her about so many things regarding her finances, her will, her wishes – where was everything? As we dug through all of Ruth's papers, we also realized we were in uncharted territory for knowing how to proceed with her affairs, what role Sara was legally allowed to play, how to handle upcoming funeral arrangements.

For example, we weren't sure whom Ruth had retained as an attorney. When we came up with the name, we heard that he had recently retired. We went to his office. What a sight when we walked in – the place was nearly empty! Staff was doing their final cleanup; the office was one hour away from shutting down for good!

We learned that Ruth's paperwork had been transferred to another law firm. We traveled there, where stacks upon stacks of boxes had arrived from the prior lawyer's office. After we told our story, an attorney started digging around in the back room, hoping to find Ruth's files. Amazingly, Ruth's paperwork was near the top of the first box! We certainly felt God's hand upon us that day.

Throughout this phase, we prayed for God to put trustworthy people in our path, to offer his kindness through others, praying for Him and for knowledgeable people to guide us. We were trusting God's provision through others, and our trust was justified.

In the town of Frankfort, Indiana, there were so many people we had to trust while there and when we returned home to our state:

- That attorney who happened to be available and dug around in the back room was perfect for us in the long run. She knew the details of state law and was experienced in the entire process for handling estates, including taxes.

- The funeral director who not only did a marvelous job, but also recommended a realtor for the house.
- The realtor who recommended an estate auctioneer.
- We could even rely on a trustworthy yard man who mowed Ruth's yard regularly while we were away.

You can feel uneasy, trusting people you don't know. I want to emphasize that trusting others doesn't mean that we didn't ask questions, or we trusted blindly. It doesn't mean that we never explored options or pushed back or even switched providers if necessary, as we did after Sara's fourth suicide attempt. But it does mean that we believed we were always being led by God into the right direction as we prayed for guidance and prayed for wise, skilled people to work with us so we could address The Next Thing.

Wise people can help you based not only on a degree or a work specialty, but from their own lived experience. You find such people when you experience a crisis where others have gone before. A couple of examples: Receiving a terminal diagnosis, and experiencing addiction (either your own or a loved one's).

In such cases, there are guides available in support groups. Even if many participants are not true guides in the purest sense, they are fellow sojourners who have guidance to offer. I urge you to find people within support groups who seem to be God's representatives sent to you to help with your crisis.

To summarize this section, God provides people to help you with the details of the Next Thing. A friend taught me to pray for God to be in all the details. We trust that the Next Thing is under God's care, that indeed, He is in all the details.

Practical Faith Principle: Gain Control by Trusting

There is a key principle at work in this section, one that another friend of ours suggested:

> **You lose control in a crisis; yet your choice to trust is something you can control.**

This next story is not about a crisis per se, but it was a journey filled with Next Things. Possibly the greatest trust Sara and I ever placed in God was when we decided to add to our family by adopting a daughter from China.

In a future chapter, I'll share the story of why we adopted. Here, I want to share the journey and process of adopting, and the trust it required.

When we first decided to adopt, we had to save money. For various reasons, it seemed like we couldn't get that adoption fund going. Different things came up, and after about a year, we still didn't have a fund. It looked like adoption was not going to happen.

Sara and I prayed about this. We prayed, "Lord, our hearts are open to adopt, but we can't seem to make it happen on our own. If you want us to adopt, then you're going to have to show us the money!"

Miraculous things started happening when we trusted the details to God. I got a promotion at work. I received consecutive raises and bonuses within a six-month period; that <u>never</u> happened at our company! An unexpected inheritance came in. Within six months, we went from having zero funds to having the tens of thousands of dollars needed for the adoption! Finally Sara and I looked at each other and said, "Well, God showed us the money! It looks like we need to go through with this!"

Fast forward through the process of deciding to adopt from China, what agency to use, and the <u>extensive</u> paperwork needed. (At one point, I commented to another father adopting from China, "Our future genealogists will have a field day with all this paperwork!" He quipped, "Or a nervous breakdown!")

It had already taken six months to acquire all the documents in the manner prescribed by the adoption agency. We finally had all the paperwork to show to an adoption lawyer who specialized in China.

She reviewed our work and finally said, "You've done a great job. You've done everything according to the guidelines of the adoption agency. But I'm sorry to tell you, the agency's instructions left out key information on the exact procedure that China requires to certify the documents. You're going to have to start all over."

Maybe that isn't the pure definition of a crisis, but it was surely a disappointing setback. We leaned on the adoption lawyer's expertise to learn exactly what we had to do, and then spent another four months assembling the correct paperwork. When we returned to her, she had more news. "China just this week changed some rules. You will have to re-do about a third of this."

It took a full year, start to finish, before the paperwork was perfect. And while it was frustrating, at the same time, we had a deep trust in the lawyer, and more importantly, a deep trust in God. We already knew that God's hands were on us, motivating us to adopt, and rather miraculously providing the money to do it when we simply couldn't find a way to save and prayed for help. We believed that every paperwork setback was designed to match us with the right daughter for our family.

When we finally headed to China with our two sons to adopt Rebecca, we had a moment that confirmed our trust.

On the first day, we had to have a family picture taken at a government office. (Here's that picture).

The workers were pointing at us and talking in Chinese. We asked our guide to translate. She said, "They're saying that every day, they see adopted children come in who don't want to leave with their new families. But in your case, they said you look like a family already!" So our trust started to be proven.

There was another element of trust I should mention. While in China, we were joined by other families adopting at the same time. Because we were adopting a three-year-old and not an infant, our family followed a different path from other families to go to her orphanage to pick her up.

This required a guide, the one I mentioned a moment ago. The guide was fantastic, knowledgeable not only in working with the orphanages, but the Chinese laws governing the special zone in which the orphanage was located. We couldn't just go to that area; we needed special permission. The guide ran interference on those procedures so that everything went smoothly start to finish. And of course, her Chinese fluency helped at every stop! (The only phrase we knew besides pleasantries was to be able to ask our new daughter, "Do you have to go to the bathroom?" That was all the conversation we could have with our little three-year-old in Chinese!)

I find our reliance on the guide to be symbolic of our need to trust a guiding God and the guides He provides to help us. We had no control of the adoption process, especially once we traveled to China. We were next to helpless in a foreign country where we didn't understand the government adoption procedures nor the language. Every day, there was a new step needed, another government office to visit, more paperwork to complete, before we were finally cleared by the US Embassy to bring Rebecca to the United States. We needed a guide!

We gained control in Rebecca's adoption by trusting – trusting in God, trusting the adoption lawyer, trusting the guide, and trusting others that He put in our path.

I feel that I should mention one more element of trust in this adoption story: the trust of a child. Rebecca not only was leaving the only home she knew, the orphanage. She cried when she left because the sights and sounds of the busy city scared her. She didn't know where she was going. She just knew us from the photos we had sent in advance, and she willingly went with us because of her trust.

Rebecca is named for two people: the stillborn daughter of friends, and the Biblical character Rebekah. The story in Genesis tells of how Rebekah willingly left her family to take an unknown husband in a strange land, trusting in God that it would work out right. It struck us as a similar story in many ways to what our Rebecca would be experiencing.

The Two Elephants in the Room

I hope I'm not making trust sound easy and consistently wonderful. I realize trust is a precious commodity. I'm asking you to do something very difficult when I ask you to trust. There are two elephants in the room I need to address:

- Trusting others in an era of mistrust
- Trusting God

Trust has been hard to come by in any era of human history, but mistrust is rampant in this century. You may find it hard to trust institutions. You may find it hard to believe what you read or hear or whatever that pesky Unknown scam caller has to say. We find it hard to even trust each other; it's possible you don't trust certain friends like you used to. Yet in the middle of mistrust, and in the midst of a crisis, I'm urging you to trust.

To trust, you must accept some level of vulnerability and risk. But if you think about it, how do you feel in a crisis in the first place? You sense the risk. You feel vulnerable.

I would again turn to the Practical Faith principle of gaining control over the Next Thing by trusting. When your world is spinning and reeling, when all is vulnerability and risk, we can slow the spinning by choosing to trust.

I'm not asking you to trust that another person is perfect and will never make a mistake; only Jesus could fulfill that requirement! Remember that I recommended you using your judgment and discernment to determine whether this is a person that God has brought to you to trust.

I started thinking about the qualities I look for when discerning whether such a person is trustworthy. I didn't literally make an official list, but this is what buzzes around in my head during a period of discernment. I look for these qualities:

- Integrity
- Listens to me
- Works with me
- Reasonable
- Competent
- Motivated
- Has my best interests at heart

You would surely add or subtract from my list. The point is, we do have to trust people every day of our lives. Look for the qualities that increase your trust in each person, so you can accept that this is a person provided by God to help you address the Next Thing.

How Can You Trust God?

The second elephant in the room is this matter of trusting God. I don't want to be flippant about this question. As Christians, we're supposed to trust God! But what is that trust based on?

Now, this topic of trusting God could be an entire lesson series or book on its own! But to very much summarize: It begins with what we learn of God in the Bible. In the Old Testament, God made big promises and kept them. Some examples:

God promised Abraham that all nations on earth would be blessed through Abraham's family – even though Abraham and Sarah were childless. Abraham had faith enough to trust God, and God delivered not only children numerous as the stars, but a Savior from the lineage of Abraham.

Later, God promised Abraham's descendants that, through Moses, he would lead them to the Promised Land. Though the journey had many twists and turns (a slalom crisis?!), God delivered.

Appearing in the New Testament as Jesus, we see more promises God kept, especially for those who trusted Him.

Jesus Heals The Epileptic Boy by Harold Copping

In the Gospel of Mark, Jesus meets a boy who had experienced muteness and convulsions most of his life. His father tells Jesus, "If you can do anything, take pity on us and help us." Jesus replies, "If you can! Everything is possible for him who believes." And in the midst of crisis, the father chooses to trust, crying out "I do believe; help me overcome my unbelief!" And Jesus heals his son.

In fact, many Gospel stories of healing are connected to the individual trusting in Jesus. That is instructive as we learn to trust God.

It is God's character to be trustworthy. That trustworthiness has been experienced by Christians for the last 2,000 years, as God's Holy Spirit has guided His church and inspired individual believers every day.

I'll have more to say shortly on what exactly a trusting person can expect from God. For now, let me turn to our core passage on trust and an extraordinary story attached to this passage.

Core Passage: Psalm 13

I haven't pretended that trusting God in crisis is easy to attain, and fortunately, in our core passage of Psalm 13, the Bible doesn't pretend, either.

Let me set up our core passage with a story. It comes from the teenage years of a woman I know, whom I'll call Katie.

In her teen years, Katie's family was very dysfunctional. Arguments between parents, and arguments between parents and children, were commonplace. Katie's parents didn't attend church, but Katie found a safe haven there. She got more and more involved in church until she was chosen to be president of the youth group.

But the level of conflict at home kept increasing. It's like Katie was living two lives, an idyllic one at church, and a torturous one at home. No one at church would've imagined what Katie was feeling inside.

One night, after yet another argument with her parents, Katie was storming around her bedroom for hours. Well after midnight, she made the fateful decision to end her life. But she was still angry, still stomping around.
In her fury, she saw a Bible. She picked it up. She yelled at it and at God, and hurled the Bible across the room, smacking the opposite wall.

As the Bible landed, it fell open in an intriguing way. Katie went over and looked. It had fallen open to Psalm 13. Katie picked the Bible up and began reading.

> **How long, O Lord? Will you forget me forever?**
> **How long will you hide your face from me?**
> **How long must I wrestle with my thoughts and every**
> **day have sorrow in my heart?**
> **How long will my enemy triumph over me?**
> **Look on me and answer, O Lord my God.**
> **Give light to my eyes, or I will sleep in death;**
> **My enemy will say, "I have overcome him," and my**
> **foes will rejoice when I fall.**

At this point in the psalm, Katie was going, "Yeah! Yeah, God! This is exactly how I feel!" Especially the part about sleeping in death; suicide was feeling very real right now.

But as Katie resumed reading Psalm 13, the psalm turned into something unexpected.

> **But I trust in your unfailing love; my heart rejoices in your salvation.**
> **I will sing to the Lord, for He has been good to me.**

That stopped Katie in her tracks. The psalmist, David, is in despair and sees no way out. He is fearful and wondering where God is in the middle of this crisis. Then he makes a choice: To keep trusting God, to trust in God's love and saving power, and to even respond with rejoicing and singing.

As she pondered all this, Katie's attitude changed. She decided not to end her life. She decided to increase her trust in God. And eventually things got better. And that whole experience set Katie on a path to choose ministry as her career.

Isn't this what we can feel in crisis? We feel abandoned, forsaken, at our wit's end, not knowing where to turn, wondering at what point God will deliver us. We may want to yell at God, but that's OK. David was mad at God. Katie was mad at God. The psalms contain numerous angry outcries to God. But as David showed, we can be angry and yet choose to trust God. As I mentioned earlier, that choice to trust gives us more control over the crisis.

Of course, we want positive outcomes, and we might question God's provision and promises when negative outcomes occur:

- The sick person dies or never fully recovers.
- The young person is taken too soon.
- The job is lost, and the next job doesn't come soon enough to limit financial ramifications.

God doesn't promise prosperity and health as much as He promises suffering. We aren't guaranteed of prayers being answered. I know a young man who stopped believing in God for a time, because he offered up prayers for good things, and none were answered. His trust in God faltered.

How do we trust God when negative outcomes occur?

Takeaways from the Bible

Let me suggest three things we can trust God to provide even when negative outcomes occur.

The first is **peace**. Paul writes in Philippians 4: 6-7:

> **Do not be anxious about anything, but in everything, by prayer and petition, with thanksgiving, present your requests to God.**

56

TRUST

And the peace of God, which transcends all under-standing, will guard your hearts and your minds in Christ Jesus.

This is an amazing statement. When we thankfully give our anxiety to God, we experience unexplainable, transcendent peace, even when circumstances don't suggest that we should feel peaceful. The peace comes in the asking, not in the outcome.

In fact, nothing in this passage says we will receive a particular outcome. Instead, the focus is on God's presence through His peace, regardless of whether we experience our desired outcome. The peace of God protects our hearts and minds and keeps us close to Christ Jesus.

Regardless of anything else that might occur when facing the Next Thing, we are within reach of God's peace by asking for help with thanksgiving, knowing God will be with us regardless of outcome.

The second thing we can count on God to provide, even in the midst of a negative outcome, is **empathy**. Empathy is different from sympathy. To sympathize with someone is to feel sorry for their pain. To empathize with someone, however, is to actually feel and understand their pain.

We CAN trust that God understands our dilemma and sits with us and weeps with us and sustains us in our desperation. We can trust God because he lived life on earth in the form of Jesus.

- Jesus is the God-who-suffers. He suffered humiliation, betrayal, loneliness.
- He experienced grief, fear, sadness and frustration.
- He was brutally beaten and experienced death in the most painful and shameful way, on a cross.

Jesus relates to everything that we go through in life, because he lived alongside us and experienced the same events we do.

[9] I really like this picture of Jesus weeping with the mourners of Lazarus. Lazarus and his family were dear friends of Jesus. Christ cried because he felt their pain, even when he knew that he was soon going to make everything all right by raising Lazarus from the dead. Jesus sat in the moment and shared their grief.

Jesus empathizes with you as you endure the ups and downs of your life, as you go through each stage of life, as you encounter your Next Things.

---

9 Photographic reproduction of "Jesus Wept" by James Tissot. This work is in the public domain in the United States and other countries/areas where the copyright term is the author's life plus 100 years or fewer.

The third thing we can trust God to provide during negative outcomes is **reclamation**. To reclaim something is to take something useless or bad, and change it for good and new purpose. God reclaims the negative event. It doesn't mean the negative outcome never happened; but God can find something positive to provide out of the negative.

[10] The best way I can describe this is with the analogy of when a landfill is transformed into a park or golf course. The landfill still contains the gunk of decades. But when reclaimed, there is something new built atop it.

I compare this to God's reclamation. There is no denying that a negative outcome has happened. The "gunk" still exists. But God can still help us build something useful atop the event and atop the pain.

In Romans 8: 28, Paul writes:

And we know that in all things God works for the good of those who love him, who have been called according to his purpose.

---

10   West, Richard. "East Lothian Landscape, Landfill and Land Reclamation at Dunbar Quarry." Usage granted under Creative Commons Attribution-ShareAlike 2.0 Generic (CC BY-SA 2.0) found at https://creativecommons.org/licenses/by-sa/2.0/deed.en .

In all things, even in negative outcomes, God works for our good, to reclaim the event for His purpose.

It might be a change of direction. It might be new wisdom, either earthly or spiritual. It might be starting a movement to address the cause of death so it doesn't happen for someone else.

I experienced reclamation during a series of extended family health crises that began with Ruth's passing. Being a caregiver or primary stakeholder in each crisis took substantial time, time that I had intended for developing Cecil Taylor Ministries. I realized that God could wait better than I could. I realized that I was best positioned in the family to address each health crisis. I experienced God's peace during prayer, telling me that I was right where I was supposed to be, and that the ministry could wait and would unfold over time. The reclamation is that those crises have become a foundation of this book and video series, "The Next Thing."

It's a mystery how good can emerge from bad. We can trust God will work to bring good out of the bad, to reclaim the damaged space and use it as the foundation for something new.

In summing up this chapter, I want to call us again to both obedience and trust during crisis. Remember the story of Peter walking on water? He could walk on water as long as he was focused on Jesus. Peter started to sink when he looked at the waves and turmoil around him.

When we are in crisis, the Bible instructs us to keep our eyes and mind on God, even as the turmoil is roiling around us. Keep your eyes on Jesus, so you won't sink. That reliance on trust is how we can peacefully experience any situation, and any crisis.

The first two parts of the Next Thing model were focused on the action verbs of Simplify and Trust. But the third part could be considered to be about inaction, as the topic is Rest. But even Rest requires intentional action, as we'll see in the next chapter.

Summary of Trust

Big Thought:
Trust that God and others will help you get through the Next Thing.

Core Passage:
Psalm 13, especially v5-6: "But I trust in your unfailing love; my heart rejoices in your salvation. I will sing to the Lord, for He has been good to me."

Practical Faith ideas:
- Prayerfully trust that God will place trustworthy individuals in front of you.
- Although you feel vulnerable and at risk, you gain control in a crisis by trusting.

Guiding thoughts for Trust, based on the Bible passages:
- We trust the trustworthy God we read about in the Bible.
- We trust that in crisis, God will provide us:
  - Peace regardless of circumstance
  - Empathy for our condition
  - Reclamation of the circumstance to make good come out of it

Rest

The breaking point was predictable. It was going to be a long, rough day, and I knew a breaking point was coming.

After Sara's mother Ruth had passed away in Indiana, and the funeral service was over, and our adult children had returned home, and we had closed down the house, Sara and I traveled to Ruth's burial in a tiny Iowa town.

I was driving a rental truck with the possessions we were keeping, while Sara drove the family car. It was a 6-hour drive to the cemetery along open interstates and through the urban traffic of Chicago.

Logically, after the mid-afternoon burial service, we should have driven a few more hours on toward western Iowa to meet Interstate 35 and turn south toward home. Instead, I had arranged to double back 30 minutes to the nearest city and a comfortable suite hotel for the night.

The funeral director was surprised. It would cost us extra time on the way home. But I knew what I was doing.

By the time our convoy arrived at the suites, Sara pulled up, shut the car off, and announced, "I'm done." My plan had worked. I knew that after such a rough day physically and emotionally, she was going to need rest, not a strenuous extra driving task for a few more hours.

A crisis can put you on the path of going, going, going. So many "Next Things" come at you. In fact, you may think the "Next Things" have exhausted themselves, and then comes another. All that makes it even more important to Rest, so you are ready for the next thing.

What does it mean to rest during crisis? Why must we rest? What is meaningful rest? How can we fit it in? These are questions I want to begin to answer in this chapter.

A Sinister Crisis

Thus far I've primarily used Ruth's passing and Sara's depression as examples for Practical Faith lessons. I want to introduce you to a third crisis within my family, when a loved one began suffering from progressive dementia, and their caregiver felt the impact.

You may recall from an earlier chapter that I said some crises have parallel tracks of Next Things. This is a great example of such a crisis.

In this case, dementia was a crisis, a Next Thing to deal with, but this sinister disease had not changed much over a period of time.

Suddenly, the loved one exhibited a startling, curious loss of capability, of physical function of their body. The caregiver had to focus on functional loss as the Next Thing. The dementia didn't go away, but the caregiver could not prioritize it as highly.

After a few weeks, an infection set in and caused life-threatening sepsis that required several weeks in the hospital and rehabilitation facilities. The infection caused bodily functions to become more impaired. These were clearly two serious Next Things, but again, the dementia, in third position, didn't go away. In fact, it worsened because of the confusing changes, moving from one medical facility to another and spending weeks away from home. Note that the caregiver was doing nothing wrong; it's just that more urgent conditions were receiving the highest priority.

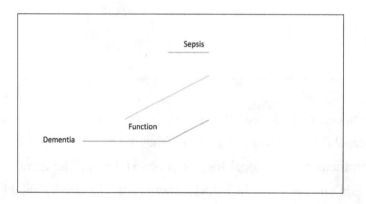

Once the sepsis was conquered, the loved one was left with even less mobility and bodily function, and by then the dementia had worsened. The caregiver could prioritize the dementia more highly, but the functional loss was still more severe. The caregiver had multiple tracks of Next Things to juggle, and the dementia had been becoming a bigger problem in the background.

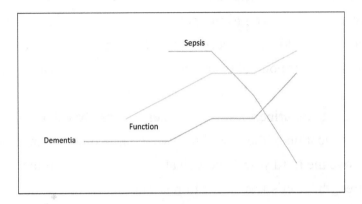

Now I want to tie these parallel tracks into our topic of Rest. From the caregiver perspective, having to address multiple Next Things left them with little time to rest, yet a growing need to rest. The caregiver was ignoring the Rest even more than the dementia. But like the dementia, things were coming to a head. The caregiver may have a breakdown of some kind if they don't have time to rest.

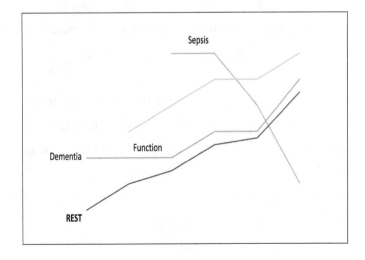

We certainly need Rest during a crisis. We can easily become overwhelmed, even to the point of exhaustion, if we're not careful. No doubt, we need to find Rest on an ongoing basis, not just at the point of breakdown. But how do we go about it?

I want to describe a four-part model for Rest, based on Jesus' identification of the first of the two greatest commandments: "Love the Lord your God with all your heart, soul, mind and strength." Let's learn how to rest our hearts, our souls, our minds and our strength!

Practical Faith Principle: Rest Your Heart through Labeling Emotions and Solitude

Resting your heart means resting your emotions. The first technique that helps rest your emotions is what I call labeling. We can feel so many emotions during a crisis: Fear, worry, anger, regret. The first step to dealing with them is labeling.

Labeling emotions is a way to identify, acknowledge and address emotions. Let me give you an example.

During a recent crisis, my key to starting to rest was to admit I was angry. I seemed patient on the outside, but on the inside, I was churning, and I really didn't know why. I finally identified – labeled – that I was angry. I didn't want to be angry, I didn't want to admit that I was angry, but I was. It was a big relief to just recognize that I was angry, give it a name, and then I could start to deal with it better.

It may sound strange to say that I didn't know I was angry, but from your own experience in crisis, perhaps you can relate. We may have a swirl of emotions. It can be useful to stop and label the emotions we're feeling, and then we can address them.

It turns out that my amateur idea of "labeling" emotions is well-observed within the field of psychology. A 2014 study found that deficits in emotional clarity were associated with symptoms of depression, social anxiety, borderline personality, binge eating, and alcohol use.[11]

On the other hand, labeling emotions helps us regulate them better. For example, if my co-worker messed something up, and I'm only aware of the anger his mistake makes me feel, I might think that I'm justified in lashing out at him. But if I happen to be aware that my emotional response also includes anxiety about having to fix this issue, I might be more motivated to downregulate my anger so that I can recruit his help.

In this second scenario, our relationship remains strong, and we effectively work together to solve problems. Thus, making an effort to understand our emotions in nonjudgmental ways can be quite valuable in terms of helping us regulate them better, and consequently, navigate our environments more smoothly.[12]

---

11 Vine, Vera and Aldao, Amelia. "Impaired Emotional Clarity and Psychopathology: A Transdiagnostic Deficit with Symptom-Specific Pathways through Emotion Regulation." Journal of Social and Clinical Psychology, April 2014.

12 Aldao, Amelia. "Why Labeling Emotions Matters." https://www.psychologytoday.com/us/blog/sweet-emotion/201408/why-labeling-emotions-matters

My second recommendation for resting our emotions is solitude. Solitude is a spiritual discipline of finding time for yourself, by yourself. During a crisis, solitude can be hard to come by. It would be ideal to find long stretches of solitude to address our emotions. But often, you have to carve out smaller amounts of time when you find them.

My best way of finding solitude is to take a walk. In fact, my wife Sara knows that I am stressed when I suddenly want to take a walk, and she never objects to that time of solitude.

I can get a lot of rest during a walk. Sometimes I'm doing some self-talk and sorting out my mind and emotions. At other times, I am getting away from the situation, experiencing nature and exercise and trying to empty my emotions.

Another way for me to sort through emotions in solitude is to shut the door and simply lie down. Maybe I'll sleep, maybe I won't, but my mind seems to operate differently in that position. Lying down gives me greater clarity in my thinking and in my emotional management.

Practical Faith Principle: Rest Your Soul through Prayer and Spirit Connection

The second attribute to rest is our soul, meaning our spirit. The two ideas here are prayer and Spirit connection, which are similar but not exactly the same thing, so I've separated them.

Prayer – of course, prayer. I could spend a lot of time on the theology of prayer, especially in a crisis, and whether we get what we pray for, and how that does or doesn't affect our view of God, and so on. But I'm talking about prayer as a tool for resting our souls. How does that work?

Earlier we read Paul's instruction to give our anxieties to God in order to receive peace. Peter echoes this in 1 Peter 5: 7:

Cast all your anxiety on him because he cares for you.

At times, I will enter a pre-bedtime meditation and prayer routine. One phase is where I literally hand off everything I'm worried about to God. In fact, in my mind, I don't even get to the point of handing each individual item to God; that can actually increase my stress as I examine each item during the handoff. Instead, my image is that I simply drop everything on the floor at His feet, telling Him, "I need to rest. Please take care of all of this until morning, and then I'll pick it up again."

It's important to note that this kind of prayer happens in an atmosphere of caring – my love for God, and more importantly, God's overwhelming love for me. It would be one thing to drop all my worries in front of a genie under my command and wish them away or order him to handle them in my absence. Instead, in an atmosphere of caring, I know God has compassion on me as I wear out. He wants me to rest,

71

wants me to be unburdened, wants me to be restored for the new day. We have a common goal.

We can also rest our spirit by connecting to the Holy Spirit. This Spirit Connection can occur either during prayer or outside of prayer. As Jesus said in Matthew 11: 28:

Come to me, all you who are weary and burdened, and I will give you rest.

I can't tell you how many times I have found comfort and rest in this verse through the Holy Spirit.

[13] To describe this kind of connection, I'll turn to Greek mythology for an analogy. When Hercules fought the giant Antaeus, he noticed that every time he threw Antaeus to the ground, Antaeus came back stronger. This is because Antaeus was gathering strength by connecting to his mother Gaia, or Mother Earth. When Hercules realized this, he defeated Antaeus by

---

13 Albiati, Ulisse. "Villa_medicea_di_Castello_-_Hercules_and_Antaeus_03". Usage granted by cyberuly under Creative Commons Attribution-ShareAlike 3.0 Unported found at https://creativecommons.org/licenses/by/3.0/legalcode .

holding him off the ground so that Antaeus was weakened and eventually crushed.

The similarity is that when we are thrown down by crisis, we can rest in, and be strengthened by, our connection to the Holy Spirit.

When we feel separated from the Holy Spirit, we feel weaker. We're strengthened by connection. Fortunately, the Spirit is always with us. It's a matter of us opening up to the Spirit.

Carving out space for rest, silence, reflection allows the Spirit to reach out to us. I think of a time when my parents separated. My father was alone in the empty house, wife and kids gone, sitting at the kitchen table and idly playing with a snow globe. This particular snow globe had a little man in a winter scene. My father would repeatedly shake it and watch the snow settle. Eventually a voice came to him, saying, "Little man, everything is cloudy and mixed up now. Eventually the snow will settle, and all will be clear to you." That gave my father strength to face the challenges ahead.

Practical Faith Principle: Rest Your Mind through Being in the Present and Rejuvenation

Now let's turn to resting our mind, which means getting relief from our thoughts, especially our preoccupied, stressful thoughts. There are many techniques for resting our minds;

one that can be controversial in Christian circles is meditation. The first technique I'll share is focusing on the present. The other is mind rejuvenation.

Focusing on the present has worked well for me. It's part of that nighttime routine I mentioned. When I say to focus on the present, I mean this very moment.

I noticed that when my mind is racing, especially in the middle of the night, it's because I'm either fretting about the past, or worrying about the future in some way. To regain control, I try to only focus on the present, what is around me right now, the activities, the sounds or the quiet. If another thought comes to my mind, I evaluate whether it is past, present or future, and I discard anything not of this moment. I've found this effective in clearing my mind of other thoughts, as not much is usually going on in the present moment, so there's little to think about.

I've written about emptying our minds, discarding our worries. But there is a counter technique, rejuvenation, which is to fill our minds with something else.

Of course, we think of filling with the word of God or the presence of the Spirit. There are alternatives, good gifts that we have available to us that we can focus on while dealing with the Next Thing.

For example, during a recent crisis, I decided to pick up my saxophone again. I worked on difficult songs with new techniques that I had never attempted before. I was not, and am still not, achieving perfection. But it has been rejuvenating to get away from stress, attempt something different and absorbing, invigorating my mind in a way that is actually restful, in terms of giving myself a break from the stress of the Next Thing.

One might call that escapism, which has its place. I'm thinking of something more riveting to rejuvenate our minds, to give us a sense of good feeling, not only a sense of getting away.

What would that look like for you? What can you do to rejuvenate your mind and feel better about yourself? Some might find rejuvenation in reading or education. An absorbing hobby. Service to others – getting outside of yourself all together and focusing on the feelings of others.

Another path to rejuvenation might be through implementing the next topic's advice.

Practical Faith Principle: Rest Your Strength through Exercise and Sleep

Finally, as we conclude this tour of resting heart, soul, mind and strength, resting our strength means resting and repairing our bodies so we can function at high capacity during crisis. I recommend both exercise and sleep.

The problem is that both are difficult during a crisis. If we're pressed for time, we cut out exercise. If we're stressed, we can have difficulty going to sleep or staying asleep. When I'm in a crisis, it's not unusual for me to wake up in the middle of the night and stay awake for awhile, fretting about the problem.

When I advocate for exercise and sleep, I'm getting into an arena where people devote entire videos and books to just those topics. I won't repeat any particular techniques, but I will urge you to actually increase your exercise and increase your sleep during a crisis.

I have found this for myself in recent years. For example, since I track my exercise, I discovered that during the crisis-filled year of 2021, I actually set my all-time record for number of workouts in a year. No doubt, exercise helped me recover my strength during the crisis.

Sleep is also important for recovery. When going through a recent crisis, I found I was sleeping less and feeling more frazzled. I decided not to simply return to my normal level of sleep, but to rearrange to sleep more than my norm! I began resting better and had more energy by increasing my normal amount of sleep.

A role model for sleep is LeBron James. In his age 37 season, James averaged 30.3 points per game, which is unprecedented for an older athlete. How does he continue to dominate younger NBA players? One of his keys to success is sleep. His teammates tease James that he only sleeps and plays basketball, as he is known to sleep 12 hours in a day!

I'm not saying you need that much sleep, but I recommend in a crisis to try to increase your sleep by, say, 30 minutes each day.

Biblical Role Models for Rest

The Bible is full of reminders and even commands that we must rest. Let me take you through a quick circuit before I turn to our core passage for Rest.

Our role model for rest is God Himself, who rested on the seventh day in the creation story and authorizes Sabbath rest in the third of the Ten Commandments.

We see rest in the exodus story as the Hebrews traveled from slavery to the Promised Land. In Exodus 33, God promises Moses that He will be present on the journey and will give rest to Moses and the people.

Once the people enter the Promised Land under Joshua's guidance, there is a busy period of fighting war and establishing territory. By Joshua chapter 21, the Lord has given the Israelites rest by providing peace on every border.

In the Psalms, which seem to contain every emotion and every type of engagement with God, rest is also described in that relationship. David sings in Psalm 62: "Find rest, O my soul, in God alone; my hope comes from him." [14]

Psalm 91 reads, "He who dwells in the shelter of the Most High will rest in the shadow of the Almighty."

There are several Gospel stories of Jesus seeking rest, whether sleep, or getting away from crowds to rest, or simply pausing a journey to rest and quench his thirst. After all, He was human and needed rest!

One example: Mark 4 describes the time when Jesus was sleeping through a storm on a sea journey while the disciples panicked. He awakens to calm the sea and the storm. Then presumably, Jesus goes back to sleep! Talk about resting during crisis!

---

14   David's Joy Over Forgiveness; as in Psalm 32; illustration from a Bible card published by the Providence Lithograph Company, 1903. In public domain in the United States.

Another example from the Gospel of Mark: At the start of Mark 6, we see Jesus sending out His disciples in pairs to reach and heal.

Later in the chapter, they return. The scripture says that so many people were coming and going that the disciples did not even have a chance to eat. So Jesus tells them, "Come with me by yourselves to a quiet place and get some rest." It's as if Jesus knew the disciples were nearing their breaking point.

I like what Pastor H.B. Charles, Jr. wrote about this verse:

> **This is a wonderful picture of the concern, gentleness, and wisdom of Jesus. After the disciples told him all they did and taught, Jesus did not grade their efforts. He did not use this as an opportunity to teach and train the disciples. And the Lord did not immediately give them their next ministry assignment. Jesus was most concerned about the toll their ministry efforts had on them. So he bid them to get away from the crowd, retreat to a quiet place, and rest from their labors.[15]**

In the midst of crisis, we may want to evaluate our efforts. We may want to immediately go and do the next thing. But instead, we need to periodically rest and regroup.

15 Charles, Jr., H.B. https://hbcharlesjr.com/resource-library/articles/come-away-and-rest-awhile/

I'm thinking of a caregiver day that was so bad, I actually noted the date: May 19, 2021. I was in the midst of caregiving for Sara after a surgery. People were telling me to take care of myself, and I would nod, and I would rest a little. But then the craziness accelerated, and I wasn't rested and prepared.

It was an ugly day. I snapped at people; I even yelled at a customer in my high tech job! That night, I stayed awake all night angry at others and then angry at myself for being angry at others and not controlling it better.

Jesus saw this in His disciples. They didn't even have a chance to eat! They were tired from their journeys, and yet there was constant craziness in the crowds around Jesus. He predicted a breaking point and pulled them away from the situation.

Think about a crisis you have experienced. What did you do with the opportunity for at least a brief rest? Did you embrace it or reject it?

One thing about crises or even very busy times is that you can get hooked on the adrenaline of activity. Your thinking changes. You find yourself looking for the next urgent task to accomplish. Simplifying helps, but that's different from what I'm talking about. In crisis, you can start chasing tasks. And instead of catching your breath and resting, you seek another task.

In the two years prior to writing this series, I faced a lot of crises. And eventually, friends started checking in on me more and more. Their main focus was on me, how was I holding up, how was I taking care of myself, how was I resting. Thank God for friends like that, because it sometimes takes that outside voice to steer you toward rest.

But I've also had an inner voice steering me toward rest and renewal. And that voice likes to quote our core scripture passage for this chapter.

Core Passage: Isaiah 40: 31

Countless times, I have awakened and felt tired even after sleep, as I know a major day is ahead of me. I have rested, but it's not enough. I'm weary but still must serve. And I have heard and cited this passage, Isaiah 40: 31, to start my day and prayed for it to be true in my life.

> **But those who hope in the Lord will renew their strength. They will soar on wings like eagles; they will run and not grow weary, they will walk and not be faint.**

This passage literally gets me out of bed. Then it seems like I always feel God's strength helping me through such a day.

In a crisis, there is so much waiting that may be needed. Time waiting for the doctor to arrive. Time waiting for results. Time waiting for a decision from a judge or an adjuster or a benefits administrator or someone choosing whether to continue a relationship. Time waiting for healing to begin and to complete.

But in a crisis, there is also a time to wait – to wait upon the Lord. To set aside our own efforts. To let God take over in your absence. To rest and to wait and to renew your heart and soul and mind and strength. And then to mount up with wings like eagles.

If you were to see an area filled with birds when a storm approaches, you would see two distinct reactions between an eagle and all other feathered creatures. While other birds would try to flee or hide, eagles would take off, in the direction of the dark clouds. Fearlessly, the eagle would fly into the fierce winds, using the storm current to rise higher quickly. The pressure of the storm is used to help them glide without using their energy as their wings' unique design allows them to lock in a fixed position amid the violent storm winds.[16]

Eagles take the storm head on, using the storm's energy and air currents to sail higher, above the worst winds, soaring over the storm to calmer air, above and beyond the storm.

---

16 Holbrook, Patricia. Atlanta Journal-Constitution, August 1, 2019.

REST

As Christians, we can soar over the storm of crisis with the uplifting, renewing power of God, a renewal that starts with rest.

For example, one time, not during a crisis but during a very busy, tiring and even overwhelming time of serving others, the Spirit presented me with a vision of being a vessel, poured out for others. And the Spirit showed me that when my vessel was empty, He would fill me up again, to be poured out again.

This is a way I have felt God renewing me and lifting me up on eagle's wings.

Maybe now is a good time to admit something, and perhaps you realize it already: I don't especially like to rest. Oh, sure, I'm good at taking short naps or resting for brief spells. But I don't like to be inactive. Sara calls me the Energizer Bunny, because I'm always moving, always going. I have lived much of my life, disdaining rest.

But I have had to teach myself to rest. Particularly during the last couple of years of constant crisis in my family, I've had to build in more intentional rest. The reason is that I can burn out, not so much physically as much as mentally, emotionally, and spiritually.

Maybe it's obvious that we all need rest during a crisis. What may not be intuitive is that we should grieve, not only after a crisis, but during it. We'll discuss this component of the Next Thing model in the next chapter.

Summary of Rest

Big Thought:
Rest, so you are ready for the Next Thing.

Core Passage:
Isaiah 40: 31: "But those who hope in the Lord will renew their strength. They will soar on wings like eagles; they will run and not grow weary, they will walk and not be faint.

Practical Faith ideas:
- Rest our hearts (emotions) through labeling emotions and solitude.
- Rest our souls (spirits) through prayer and Spirit connection.
- Rest our minds (thoughts) through being in the present and rejuvenation.
- Rest our strength (bodies) through increased exercise and sleep.

Guiding thoughts for Rest, based on the core passage:
- The Lord helps us to overcome weariness and empowers us to fly again into the face of our storms.

Grieve

It was like a slow-motion car wreck, watching but unable to stop what was happening. The telecom startup company where I was second-in-command was on a path to folding, because the boss wasn't listening to me anymore, and he was running the company aground.

Two years earlier, I had committed myself to a technology startup, taking less salary along with future promises, to help build a company. Despite the pains to launch, it was going great! I finished my online MBA in Corporate Entrepreneurship while working at the startup. I felt so rewarded, because it seemed like every day, I was learning something in MBA class that I applied to the company, increasing our success.

We were making a mark, getting ahead of competition, building up a client base. Competitors were already making offers to buy us out. Everything was pointing up…

…until the boss decided to go a different direction, one that held promise, but was way beyond our little company's capabilities. Everything I had learned from my MBA told me it would fail.

Three times over a period of months, I staged interventions with the owner to try to convince him to return to what was making us successful. I would have bad dreams throughout the night of the company failing. I offered alternatives to at least keep the company going on revenue-generating tasks while he isolated the new work from what was making us go. But he was insistent on staying his ill-fated course.

So I was already grieving the dream, grieving what could have been, long before the layoff notice arrived.

A crisis usually means the end of something. And with the end of something comes grief. Grief stems from a loss.
- Loss of a job.
- Loss of a relationship.
- Loss of a loved one who has passed away.
- Loss of a home we loved, maybe due to finances, maybe due to fire or natural disaster. And in that case, there may be much more than a home that was lost.

- Loss that comes from the inevitable change in life, such as returning to a place we loved and finding it different or gone.
- Loss of a dream.

That's what happened when I lost my startup job. It was more than a job. It was a dream, to have such influence, to help the company grow, to create the possibility of eventually selling the company for great reward. It was a satisfying time, and then it ended. And while I moved on, I have never fully gotten over it.

In this chapter of The Next Thing, I want to describe the practical aspect of grieving during crisis before sharing the Bible story of someone who grieved during crisis themselves. Along the way, I'll share a framework for grief and explore how we can accept new realities and move on as best as possible.

Saying Goodbye Bit by Bit

Let me explain my approach to this topic of grieving during crisis. Now, grief itself is too big of a topic for a chapter – it's a book! I'm reminded of proposing a topic for a research paper in high school. I told my teacher I would write on the Gettysburg Address. She said, "That's a book, not a research paper! Instead, find some smaller aspect of the Gettysburg Address and research that."

Similarly, my purpose here isn't to comprehensively explain grief. I do want to introduce some grief concepts, based on academic models, and then show why and how to apply them in the midst of crisis, rather than only when the crisis has passed.

I'll start by returning to a family crisis from the prior lesson, when a loved one suffered from dementia.

 To remind you of the imagery from the opening lesson, dementia is a slalom-type of crisis, with many twists and turns, many Next Things. A friend whose mother had dementia described the disease as a winding staircase that gradually descends, with different levels of function. However, some sections are more like steep slides. Dementia takes away a person, a bit at a time.

Each level is a level of function or awareness that is not reclaimed, not ascended again. In the midst of it, as a caregiver or as a family member looking on, you may find yourself grieving in stages as the person's functions or attributes disappear.

As I described in the Rest chapter, our family was seeing our loved one with dementia losing physical function and mobility, as well as seeing mental capacity and personality eroding.

As family members experienced these phases, I helped them identify in their stress that we were truly grieving already. We were grieving that we did not have the person we once had, missing them already. We were grieving opportunities lost, activities we used to do together, conversations we used to have, memories we used to share.

Grieving during the crisis really helped family members to say goodbye to functions and attributes one by one, to adapt better to each new normal, each Next Thing, to accept the reality of the disease rather than fighting it.

More difficult but similarly, how does one grieve their own life in a health crisis? It may not be clear what functions and vitality can be restored and what is lost. One always needs hope and a fighting spirit, and at the same time, the reality may be that certain functions and vitality are no longer possible.

Later, I'll share a practical faith principle, Live the Life that is Given, that will help address this topic.

Back to my opening story about my dream job, I had a period of about nine months to grieve the inevitable loss of my job. I found myself in a mixed position of fighting to change things while otherwise sitting in a stunned stupor, hoping against hope that the boss was right, but helpless to change the outcome. If I had to do it all over again, I would have gotten over my inaction sooner and started hunting for the next job. I didn't know it, but a major recession was around the corner, and by waiting until the bitter end, I wound up being underemployed for the next 14 months.

But I did indeed grieve during the last nine months of employment. The "bit by bit" was watching one loyal customer after another disappear because we weren't servicing them correctly anymore; trying to acquire new sales opportunities that were so close, but we couldn't commit, and the prospect would leave us; and feeling the loss of the close, synergistic relationship I once had with the boss. By the time my layoff came, the company was a shell of its former self, and a lot of my grieving had already been accomplished.

Let's turn now to three practical faith principles related to grieving during a crisis.

Practical Faith Principle: Accept the Loss Realistically, Directly and Responsibly

I really thought about what word to use here to describe this adaptation to each Next Thing. I've chosen the word "acceptance," for a couple of reasons. First, acceptance doesn't mean that we like or enjoy the Next Thing. It means we acknowledge the reality and adapt.

David Kessler wrote:

Acceptance is often confused with the notion of be-ing 'all right' or 'OK' with what has happened. This

is not the case. Most people don't ever feel OK or all right...Finding acceptance may be just having more good days than bad ones. As we begin to live again and enjoy our life, we often feel that in doing so, we are betraying our loved one. We can never replace what has been lost, but we can make new connections, new meaningful relationships, new inter-dependencies.[17]

The second reason for using the word "acceptance" is that it is part of the most widely used grieving model, which was first identified by Elisabeth Kubler-Ross. Psychologists have tried to label grief in stages as a way of understanding and getting through it. Kubler-Ross was a founder of such labeling, starting with 5 stages and later adding a sixth. The stages are:

- Denial
- Anger
- Bargaining
- Depression
- Testing how to regain control – *that was the new phase she added*
- And finally, Acceptance [18]

Acceptance can mean several things, but what I'm leveraging is that it can be engaging with reality as it is, and adapting, coping and responding skillfully to that reality.

---

17 Kessler, David. https://grief.com/the-five-stages-of-grief/

18 Kubler-Ross, Elisabeth and Kessler, David. *On Grief and Grieving: Finding the Meaning of Grief Through the Five Stages of Loss.* New York: Scribner, 2014.

eCondolence.com points out three things about acceptance:

1. Acceptance honestly looks at the new reality.
2. Acceptance doesn't ignore the loss.
3. Acceptance takes responsibility

As stated above, you may never feel OK or right about the loss. **Honestly looking at the new reality** simply means you realize the loss can't be changed. eCondolence.com posted:

> **Acceptance also does not mean forgetfulness. Acceptance does not mean that we slip back into denial – pretending that it has not or will not happen. Acceptance means embracing the present – both good and bad – in order to shape the future.**[19]

"Embrace" may seem like an odd word to use. Embracing implies openness and is an act of will. We decide to accept the new reality instead of ignoring or avoiding it. So we directly look at the new reality, then we embrace the new reality.

The second aspect of acceptance is that we **don't ignore the loss**. This doesn't mean that we either forget or deny the loss.

Humans tend to avoid problems instead of tackling them. M. Scott Peck wrote about this pain avoidance:

> **Fearing the pain involved, almost all of us, to a greater or lesser degree, attempt to avoid problems.**

19 https://www.econdolence.com/learning-center/grief-and-coping/the-stages-of-grief/fifth-stage-of-grief-acceptance/

We procrastinate, hoping that they will go away. We ignore them, forget them, pretend that they do not exist. We even take drugs to assist us in ignoring them, so that by deadening ourselves to the pain, we can forget the problems that caused the pain. We attempt to skirt around problems instead of taking them head on. We attempt to get out of them rather than suffer through them….But the substitute itself ultimately becomes more painful than the legitimate suffering it was designed to avoid.[20]

Peck goes on to recommend that we teach ourselves and our children the necessity for and the value of suffering. We need to face problems directly, experience the pain involved, then move past the pain and suffering. This is opposite of ignoring the loss.

Peck's excerpt also applies to the third principle to **take responsibility**. We're responsible for ourselves, responsible for our actions. We take ownership of moving toward a more normal life.

Combined, these three aspects of acceptance shape the new normal – new roles, responsibilities, priorities, relationships. We take on new tasks and relationships but may also shed other tasks and relationships.

---

20 Peck, M. Scott, *A Road Less Traveled: A New Psychology of Love, Traditional Values and Spiritual Growth.* New York: Simon & Schuster, 1979.

In my context of grieving during a crisis, acceptance means that we pivot during the crisis. We recognize what has changed, grieve its loss, and strive to accept the Next Thing so we can move forward and act on that Next Thing.

Using the dementia example, one of the things I worked on with family members is that the new normal kept changing, that Next Things were happening more frequently. Family members were sometimes stuck with old perceptions, old information, even old misgivings about the person. In this role, I kept showing that things had changed, that these old perceptions, information and misgivings were irrelevant now. This undoubtedly was valuable as it kept the family members on the same page, able to move on to the Next Thing, even as we individually and collectively mourned those changes.

Practical Faith Principle: Live the Life that is Given

One of the best examples I've seen of acceptance, one of the stoutest approaches, came from a 13-year-old girl who died of cystic fibrosis. After her passing, her mother found a diary entry her daughter had written. It said:

I will live the life that is given.[21]

I will live the life that is given. What a powerful phrase, what a powerful attitude displayed by this young victim! She accepted

---

21 Matousek, Mark. https://www.goodhousekeeping.com/health/wellness/advice/a18937/how-to-handle-a-crisis/

her situation in a way that followed and summarized the prior Practical Faith Principle:

- It wasn't that she liked it, but she was honest about her reality.
- She didn't ignore the loss, but directly faced it, embracing what life she did have.
- She took responsibility for her attitude and actions.

In doing so, I can only imagine that her life was enriched, that her faith helped her live vibrantly as far as she was capable, that she lived with gratitude rather than regret.

This is a marvelous phrase to embed into our lives and our souls, and the more I ponder it, the more I love it. Life is a gift from God, even with its remarkable highs and lows, joy and sorrow, and all the Next Things we must face. In fact, life can sometimes seem to merely be a series of Next Things. But if we focus on living the life that is given, we can address problems of change and grief and more, and live an enriched, vibrant, grateful life.

This principle addresses several specific situations that come to mind. Obviously, as this wisdom came from a young woman looking at her own compromised position, I feel it can apply for those who through age or illness have lost function and vitality. The motto of living the life that is given could give new perspective to your situation.

For those in difficult, crisis-filled family situations, this motto could be an anchor in dealing with them. For example, a spouse or child or parent of an alcoholic or addict can feel many moments of despair and helplessness. For those who decide to stay in relationship and help despite setbacks and disappointments, there are periods of simply living the life that is given. Perhaps things will get better or worse, but to stay in the moment and live the life that is given can get you through the day.

I think of how this concept applies to my chapter-opening story about the startup company. Clearly at some point I had to let go and move on. Interestingly, after I was laid off, I wound up doing some contract work for the company before moving on entirely. I was not very hopeful that I would be able to return, but the company still owed me money, so I was hoping that a turnaround could happen.

I secured the next job, but the new role offered a very different environment, one that I actually did not like and considered one of my worst workplaces ever. In less than two years, I had resigned and found a better role for me.

As it turned out, the work life that was given in the new and better role still leveraged the learning from the startup. It still leveraged my MBA in new ways. It tapped into the competitive techniques I had learned in the startup. I carried all that with me and was excited to deploy it in new ways.

Yes, I lost the dream job. But I wound up living the dream in a different way, creating fresh ventures within my new company. Eventually I accomplished some of the biggest achievements of my career. In no small measure, my time at the startup was a factor.

Practical Faith Principle: Don't Heal; Seal

Now, I'll point out that the Kubler-Ross grief model has several issues. First, grief is not one-size-fits-all, but a very individual experience. In the dementia crisis, not every family member grieved in the same way nor at the same rate. Second, grief is not as predictable and sequential and final as the model suggests. When I talked about Rest, I emphasized that you can predict breaking points. You can't do that with grief. You can't predict grief breaking points.

Grief is like a big ocean wave that washes over you unexpectedly. You may know the potential for that wave is there, but it still catches you by surprise.

To use another analogy, you can think your feelings are packed away in a trunk, but those can spring out like a jack-in-a-box at unexpected times and with the smallest of memories.

In fact, even Kubler-Ross cautioned when she wrote:

> **The reality is that you will grieve forever. You will not 'get over' the loss of a loved one; you will learn**

to live with it. You will heal and you will rebuild yourself around the loss you have suffered. You will be whole again but you will never be the same. Nor should you be the same nor would you want to.[22]

When I saw this quote from Kubler-Ross, it made me think of something I learned about trees when developing a previous video lesson series found on CecilTaylorMinistries.com, "The Legacy Tree: A Christian Model for a Life of Significance." This series uses a tree metaphor to present a model for how to define ourselves, give ourselves and replenish ourselves in order to serve and produce significance for God's kingdom.

[23]One of the things I learned then is how a tree handles a wound through a process called compartmentalization. When a tree is wounded, the injured tissue is not repaired and does not heal. Trees do not heal; they seal. If you look at an old wound, you will notice that it does not "heal" from the inside

22 Kubler-Ross, Elisabeth and Kessler, David. *On Grief and Grieving: Finding the Meaning of Grief Through the Five Stages of Loss.* New York: Scribner, 2014.

23 Krzysztof Ziarnek, Kenraiz. Tree callus. Usage granted under Creative Commons Attribution-ShareAlike 4.0 found at https://creativecommons.org/licenses/by-sa/4.0/

out, but eventually the tree covers the opening by forming specialized "callus" tissue around the edges of the wound. After wounding, new wood growing around the wound forms a protective boundary preventing the infection or decay from spreading into the new tissue. Thus, the tree responds to the injury by "compartmentalizing" or isolating the older, injured tissue with the gradual growth of new, healthy tissue. Not only do trees try to close the damaged tissue from the outside, they also make the existing wood surrounding the wound unsuitable for spread of decay organisms.[24]

Trees do not heal; they seal. Compartmentalization allows trees to continue to grow and develop, even if they always carry the wound with them.

This is a model we can use when grieving on the go: Sealing rather than healing.

- We can feel guilty about grieving and seeming to heal. It feels like we have forgotten who or what was lost.
- Compartmentalization means if we seal, the wound is there, but with a callus on it. We also prevent the spread of the wound into other areas of our lives.
- New growth can continue, but it does not replace the wound. Injury still exists, but just like the tree, we are able to grow in new directions.

---

24 Clatterbuck, Wayne K. https://extension.tennessee.edu/publications/Documents/SP683.pdf

Sealing honors where we have been and what once was, while also allowing us to accept the new reality and focus on moving forward.

A Biblical Prequel to Grief

As we turn to scripture for support of this concept of grieving during crisis, I'm taking a different tack this time. We'll eventually look at a core passage, but I want to begin by looking across two entire books of the Bible.

The prophet Jeremiah is believed to have authored both the Book of Jeremiah and the Book of Lamentations. The Book of Jeremiah is the story of his prophecy of the destruction of Jerusalem and describes its eventual capture. Lamentations is poetry in the aftermath of that destruction.

Jeremiah prophesied for approximately 40 years before the fall of Jerusalem in 586 BC. He warned of destruction and exile due to God's judgment against the sin of the people. But he also signaled that sincere repentance would postpone the inevitable.

It's interesting that we see Jeremiah grieving in the midst of crisis. Even before Jerusalem falls, he can see the decay leading to the fall, and it makes him sorrowful. Jeremiah mourns in Jeremiah 8:21 – 9:1.

> **Since my people are crushed, I am crushed;**
> **I mourn, and horror grips me.**

Is there no balm in Gilead?
Is there no physician there?
Why then is there no healing for the wound of my people?
Oh, that my head were a spring of water and my eyes a fountain of tears!
I would weep day and night for the slain of my people.

As J. Gordon McConville put it, "Jeremiah feels already the pain that will come upon the people."[25]

Eventually that pain does come. Nebuchadnezzar and his Babylonian army march on Jerusalem. They break down the wall, burn the royal palace and people's homes, and destroy the temple. They force to Babylonian exile a subset of Jerusalem residents, the leadership, perhaps 25% of the people, while leaving the rest to fend for themselves amidst the rubble.

Core Passage: Lamentations 3: 20b-26

That brings us to Lamentations, in which Jeremiah stays in Jerusalem and laments what has happened. Now, the crisis is not over. In fact, Jerusalem is experiencing incredible suffering, the ruin of their worship pattern, and the exile of a good chunk of their population. So Jeremiah poetically laments what has happened and how the people's sin has brought this destruction upon them.

---

25 J. Gordon McConville, *Judgment and Promise: An Interpretation of the Book of Jeremiah.* University Park, PA: Eisenbraun, 1993.

Yet Jeremiah brings us to a place of hope in our core passage. He knows that God is good, and God will restore Jerusalem. It doesn't mean everything will be back as it was; Jerusalem is changed forever. But Jeremiah hopefully believes that a new Jerusalem will eventually be born out of these remnants. The core passage is from Lamentations 3: 20b-26.

> **My soul is downcast within me. Yet this I call to mind and therefore I have hope: Because of the Lord's great love, we are not consumed, for his compassions never fail. They are new every morning; great is your faithfulness. I say to myself, "The Lord is my portion; therefore, I will wait for him." The Lord is good to those whose hope is in him, to the one who seeks him; it is good to wait quietly for the salvation of the Lord.**

Doesn't it remind you of David's feelings in Psalm 13, the core passage of the Trust chapter? Jeremiah is downcast yet retains hope and trust in the Lord.

Takeaways from the Core Passage

I want to pick apart the core passage in two ways, looking at what God offers us in the midst of grief and despair, and what we are supposed to do in return. First, God's list.

- **Love**
- **Compassion**
- **Faithfulness**
- **Portion (or Presence)**

God offers **love**. As the people of Jerusalem learned the hard way, sometimes God offers tough love. But He loves us as the perfect father, knowing the right blend of grace and judgment, of tenderness and correction, so that we can be sanctified, molded into the character of Jesus.

Isn't it amazing that God still loves this disobedient people? We can feel like we don't deserve God's love, either because of our wrongdoing, or because we simply feel tiny compared to God. But God loves each of us deeply and, no matter what, is always the shepherd leaving the 99 sheep to find and reclaim the lost one.

God offers **compassion** that is fresh with every morning. His compassion never fails and never runs dry. If there is one motivator we see in Jesus in the gospels, a word that keeps coming up, it is compassion.

[26]I talk about this in "The Legacy Tree" video series, where I cite the following as examples of Jesus' compassion:

---

26 Photographic reproduction of "Healing the Leper" by Н.М.Алексеев. This work is in the public domain in the United States and other countries/areas where the copyright term is the author's life plus 100 years or fewer.

- In Mark 1:

  A man with leprosy came to him and begged him on his knees, "If you are willing, you can make me clean." Filled with **compassion**, Jesus reached out his hand and touched the man. "I am willing," he said. "Be clean!"

- In Matthew 14:

  The crowds followed him on foot from the towns. When Jesus landed and saw a large crowd, he had **compassion** on them and healed their sick.

- In Matthew 9:

  When he saw the crowds, he had **compassion** on them, because they were harassed and helpless, like sheep without a shepherd.

- In Mark 8:

  During those days another large crowd gathered. Since they had nothing to eat, Jesus called his disciples to him and said, "I have **compassion** for these people; they have already been with me three days and have nothing to eat."

- In Luke 15, in the Parable of the Prodigal Son, Jesus portrays himself as the loving father:

  But while the son was still a long way off, his father saw him and was filled with **compassion** for him; he ran to his son, threw his arms around him and kissed him.

Next, God is **faithful**. God keeps every promise and never gives up on us. That can be so hard to believe – for ourselves and for others. God is ever the prodigal's father, as shown above, waiting at the window to run to us at the first sign of repentance.

As described in the Trust chapter, God's faithfulness is a primary reason that we can trust God.

And then there's this curious phrase that the Lord is my **portion**. This is the same wording we see in Numbers 18: 20, when God tells Aaron that his priestly tribe of Levites will receive no land of their own in the Promised Land. While the other tribes will receive land, the tribe of Levi will receive God Himself as their portion of the inheritance. And God is no consolation prize; he's the biggest prize!

To say that the Lord is my portion in crisis is to say that we experience the constant, eternal presence of God. God is with us in crisis. We are not alone. Thanks be to God!

Now let's turn from God's contribution in this Lamentations equation to our contributions, which are:
- **Hope**
- **Waiting**
    - ○ **With Patience**
    - ○ **With Anticipation**

Our core passage in Lamentations 3 emphasizes that we are to **hope** – to hope in all these things that God provides (love, compassion, faithfulness, presence), and to hope that a brighter day will come, a day of restoration and renewal, just as Jeremiah hoped for a rebuilt Jerusalem.

Hope may not be the major theme of "The Next Thing," but it is a recurring one. We once again encounter it in Lamentations, just as we did in the Simplify chapter when discussing Paul's equation in Romans that suffering leads to endurance leads to character leads to hope. Hope also was a factor in the Trust chapter, as we put our hope in the One who is trustworthy.

In his poem, "An Essay on Man," Alexander Pope wrote the enduring line, "Hope springs eternal in the human breast." Perhaps it's because we are made for hope. Perhaps it's because hope is an essential part of the human story. One of my favorite Christian authors, Henri Nouwen, wrote:

> **Wiesel writes, "God made man because he loves stories." As long as we have stories to tell to each other there is hope. As long as we can remind each other of the lives of men and women in whom the love of God becomes manifest, there is reason to move forward to new land in which new stories are hidden.**[27]

---

27 Nouwen, Henri J.M. *The Living Reminder: Service and Prayer in Memory of Jesus Christ.* San Francisco: HarperOne, 1984.

I feel like this passage intimately ties into the concept of "The Next Thing." This Grieve chapter has advocated for the need to grieve while going forward, sealing our grief so that we can move forward into fresh territory. An essential part of each of our stories is moving forward, and hence an essential part of our stories is hope.

Our other action mentioned in the core passage is **waiting** for the Lord and waiting quietly for the saving action of the Lord. I think this means two things. First, we wait with **patience**. God moves in his own time and with his own wisdom, not ours. Still, we can wait patiently because of our hope and trust in God's love, compassion, faithfulness and presence.

But we combine that patience with **anticipation**. We are ready for God to move at any time. We are eager for what's next. I like the first two definitions of "anticipate" found on Dictionary.com:

1. To realize beforehand; foretaste or foresee.
2. To expect; look forward to; be sure of.

First, we realize and foresee beforehand what is going to happen, and we get a foretaste of it. Second, we expect and look forward to what will happen. In fact, we are sure of it!

So in crisis, we wait for our own "rebuilt Jerusalem" patiently but with anticipation. We know there are mounds of rubble to clean up, walls to fortify, homes to rebuild while mourning the loss of what once was. But something new is also coming, and we wait for it with patience and anticipation.

This concludes the four-part model of "The Next Thing," identifying how and why to Simplify, Trust, Rest and Grieve. Now I want to connect the dots between these concepts and give you some final thoughts in the concluding chapter.

Summary of Grieve

Big Thought:

Grieve, so you can accept and act on the Next Thing.

Core Passage:

Lamentations 3: 20b-26: "My soul is downcast within me. Yet this I call to mind and therefore I have hope: Because of the Lord's great love, we are not consumed, for his compassions never fail. They are new every morning; great is your faithfulness. I say to myself, 'The Lord is my portion; therefore I will wait for him.' The Lord is good to those whose hope is in him, to the one who seeks him; it is good to wait quietly for the salvation of the Lord."

Practical Faith ideas:

- Accept the loss realistically, directly and responsibly.
- Live the life that is given.
- Don't heal the wound; seal it to honor what was and to move forward.

Guiding thoughts for Grieve, based on the core passage:

- In the midst of grief and despair, God offers us love, compassion, faithfulness and his portion (or presence).
- In return, we hope and wait patiently and with anticipation.

Connective Tissue

I've written about the components of simplifying, trusting, resting and grieving in a crisis, but I haven't shared any connective tissue to bind them together. That's what I will do in this chapter.

In addition, I have some final thoughts about crises – how they change us and how we can view those crises as we go through time.

When I told you I had a four-part model for dealing with a crisis, I don't imagine you would've listed Simplify, Trust, Rest and Grieve as the components. As I thought about "The Next Thing," those four ideas swiftly coalesced for me. I recently reviewed my original notes for the series, and there weren't even any other candidates besides these four! I guess they just came to me naturally as I evaluated the crises of my life.

It's strange – "The Legacy Tree" video series was an on-and-off project for 20 years, with many refinements and redefinitions. By contrast, "Live Like You're Loved" settled very quickly, just like "The Next Thing." But in all three cases, the models came from my lived experience. For "The Legacy Tree," I was really trying to live a model and tweaking it and reviewing it, and that is reflected by the redefinitions. In the case of the other two, it was simply articulating what I had already done, two successful models that I had already used and believed in.

Returning to "The Next Thing" wrap-up, let me now explain the connective tissue, how I see the four elements of the model tied together.

Our Role and God's Role in Crisis

Similar to showing God's role and our role in crisis in the Grieve chapter, I feel that the overview of "The Next Thing" model would boil down to our role in a crisis and God's role in a crisis.

> **Our role: Take care of our <u>response</u> to the Next Thing.**
> **God's role: Take care of the <u>outcome</u> of the Next Thing.**

In our role, the actions of Simplify, Trust, Rest and Grieve help us respond to the Next Thing.

What enables us to respond to the Next Thing? Certainly this passage from 2 Timothy 1: 7 has broader application, but I find it useful in considering our role in responding to the Next Thing.

> **For the Spirit God gave us does not make us timid,**
> **but gives us power, love and self-discipline.**

When we are faced with the Next Thing, we do not need to be overwhelmed by it. We want to attain a gifted spirit of power, love and self-discipline.

We have power – God's power primarily, but also powerful, scripture-supported tools in Simplifying, Trusting, Resting and Grieving. We have love – God's love flowing through us to others and that we can demonstrate in the midst of crisis. We have self-discipline – the Spirit fruit of self-control, paired with this model I've discussed that also requires discipline, especially in terms of simplifying, trusting and resting.

I hope it's evident that the model to Simplify, Trust, Rest and Grieve does not necessarily change the outcome of our crisis. These components primarily govern our approach to the Next Thing at hand.

As for outcomes, there are two ways to consider how God takes care of the Next Thing.

 First, we pray for change, asking God to make the outcome better. We can take the same approach as Jesus did in Gethsemane as he prepared for the cross, in what I call the Lord's Other Prayer. We find a simple, powerful prayer in Mark 14: 36 that can also address Next Things:

> **Abba, Father, everything is possible for you. Take this cup from me. Yet not what I will, but what you will.**

I love this very succinct prayer, acknowledging God's power, making a request to God, and then accepting whatever outcome occurs.

After that prayer comes the second way to consider how God takes care of the Next Thing. We trust in God through all outcomes, as I described in the second lesson on Trust when I outlined how God provides us peace, empathy and reclamation.

- We trust that God's peace will be with us, starting with when we present our requests to God.

- We trust that God understands what it's like to face the Next Thing and to endure negative outcomes, because Jesus lived life, too, and empathizes.
- We trust God to make good emerge from bad, to reclaim the event and build atop the pain.

We are trusting that God will be present and caring in all outcomes. Even if you lived a life of only positive outcomes (ha!), there will one day be an outcome that leads to your death. God will also be present and caring in that moment and beyond. If we can trust God's providence beyond the grave, we can also trust God's providence in all the Next Things of this life.

Crisis Fundamentally Changes Us

In the opening chapter, I shared several definitions of a crisis, including that it is a turning point; a stage in a sequence of events at which the trend of future events is determined. A crisis also has great impact.

I would submit that in addition to the turning points and great impacts on various aspects of our lives, a crisis is a turning point that has a great impact on who we are. Each of us is changed by crisis in fundamental ways.

It's time to reveal some of the symbolism of the art you've seen throughout this book. If you look again at the first page of this chapter and examine "The Next Thing" art, you'll see the large ball of yarn symbolizing the Next Thing itself. It is a tangle of types and colors of yarn. But for the purpose of this chapter, I want to focus on what you see entering and exiting the Next Thing ball.

The light blue yarn symbolizes you. The white yarn symbolizes God. The black yarn symbolizes the crisis itself. Often but not always, the crisis already exists before we are aware of it. The black yarn represents the looming crisis.

Coming out of the Next Thing ball of yarn, you see these three colors persist. Other colors symbolize the confusion, the tasks, the decisions, perhaps even the people who become part of the Next Thing event. But coming out, these fall away, and what is left is you, God and the crisis, interwoven tightly.

This symbolizes how the crisis has changed you. It may be over, and yet it is part of your journey going forward.

Including God in the weave is important. Ideally the experience has brought you closer to God, or perhaps even without you knowing it, God has become as embedded as He can in your life. It's another way to express the idea of "footprints in the sand", where God carries you through the rough times.

Knowing this symbolism, I encourage you to examine the art for Simplify, Trust, Rest and Grieve in a new way.

Let me return to my assertion that crisis fundamentally changes us. It helps to understand this concept through the

118

shared crises that shift our society. Going back a century: The Depression. World War II. The JFK assassination. 9/11. The COVID pandemic. These crises fundamentally changed us as a society. Life is not the same after they've occurred. Similarly, we can be fundamentally changed by personal crisis. I'll give a couple of my own examples.

I spent a lot of my life working in the high-tech field, where it's common for companies to dramatically grow and dramatically shrink. Within a ten-year period from 2005 to 2015, I was either unemployed or under-employed for five and a half years. Not only did I have to deal with changes in finances, but my family and I underwent fundamental change. We came out of it with more gratitude for what we have. We have a deeper empathy for the poor and unfortunate. We learned flexibility and how to make it through tough times.

As Christmas rolled around during one particularly bad year, when I had lost my dream job, we were the recipients of so much generosity, including anonymous donors at our church. I remember being overwhelmed at the food and gifts presented to our family. My oldest son Anthony said, "It's the love of God, Dad."

That year we bought silver and gold ball ornaments on which we could write. We sat down together and labeled the ornaments with the things we were grateful for that year and hung them on the Christmas tree. Every year, those same ornaments go up, reminding us in times of both plenty and want that we need to be grateful for the people and the possessions that we do have. That's an example of fundamental change.

An earlier family crisis that fundamentally changed us was infertility. For five years, it was not evident that Sara and I could ever have children.

Eventually we were able to have two natural-born sons, but we were fundamentally changed. When you go through that, in your mind, you are still infertile, even after having children. When going through infertility, Sara and I seriously looked into adoption.

And our hearts remained open to adoption even after the two births. We always told Anthony and Austin that we would eventually adopt. And we did when we added Rebecca to our family. We were fundamentally changed by infertility. Without it, we likely would never have adopted Rebecca.

Crisis can fundamentally change you for better or for worse. It depends on how you react to it. I know a man whose parents divorced when he was young, and he used it as an excuse for doing a lot of bad things in his life. I know another man who used his parents' divorce to drive him to greater accomplishment and morality.

Business author Jon Acuff says a crisis is always trying to teach you something you might not have learned voluntarily.[28] If nothing else, a crisis can teach us to better love and comfort others with empathy. For example, I experienced fundamental change from infertility in another way: Empathy. When a family member went through infertility later, I was able to approach it differently. I don't think I would have been as compassionate or empathetic without my own experience. It has also helped me gain more sympathy for others' lived experiences when I have not had the same experience.

Paul talks about the empathy we gain from crisis in 2 Corinthians 1.

> **Praise be to the God and Father of our Lord Jesus Christ, the Father of compassion and the God of all comfort, who comforts us in all our troubles, so that we can comfort those in any trouble with the comfort we ourselves have received from God.**

Just as we receive God's love and can let it flow through us to others, we can go through fundamental change – for good or for bad – and still be able to let God's compassion and comfort flow through us to others.

---

28 https://www.linkedin.com/pulse/personal-crisis-changed-my-life-12-years-ago-jon-acuff/

Another Slogan to Live By

I was teaching a Sunday School class of the eldest members of our church. Well, to say I was teaching was a strong word. I was learning as much as I was teaching!

I was leading a discussion on how you get through the ups and downs of life, and some great stories were coming out. I was collecting them to use during an upcoming young adult retreat I was leading.

Then a man named Sam Farler raised his hand and told about the hardships of his life. I don't recall all the crises that Sam listed, but I do remember the list included the loss of a child and the failure of multiple businesses he owned. He used a simple phrase to explain how he got through the hardships. And just like I was underwhelmed when Leighton Farrell told me on the worst day of my life to "stay spiritually strong," I was underwhelmed when Sam recited this phrase: "This too shall pass."

Then I looked in his eyes, and I saw it all: the hardships, the wounds, the pain, the recovery, the resolution, the peace. And I understood that simple, well-known phrase in a brand new way.

The phrase itself is as old as written communication. Supposedly it came from Persia. Abraham Lincoln related the story in a speech to the Wisconsin State Agriculture Society in 1859:

> **It is said an Eastern monarch once charged his wise men to invent him a sentence, to be ever in view, and**

122

**which should be true and appropriate in all times
and situations. They presented him the words: "And
this, too, shall pass away." How much it expresses!
How chastening in the hour of pride! How consoling
in the depths of affliction!**

In the depths of affliction, through his own series of Next
Things, Sam leaned on this phrase.

Reflecting on Sam's story now, I can frame Sam's saying and
experience in terms of "The Next Thing":

- Sam was able to simplify so he could focus on the
  Next Thing.
- Sam trusted God and God's kindness through others
  to get through the Next Thing.
- Sam found rest in that phrase, even in the swirling
  storm of crisis.
- Sam grieved so he could accept and act on the Next
  Thing.

For each of us, this Next Thing shall pass, and it will pass
better, as we simplify, trust, rest and grieve our way through
it, taking care of our response to the Next Thing and trusting
God to handle the outcome of the Next Thing, even while
undergoing fundamental change kindled by the Next Thing.

May God bless you as you encounter all the Next Things in
your life!